Unfailing Love

Times

———————————

A Journey Through 1 John

By J. Ryan Wicker

ISBN: 978-1-7375838-0-6 (eBook)

ISBN: 978-1-7375838-1-3 (Paperback)

Dedicated to my wonderful wife of fifteen years, Rebekah. Your encouragement and love made this possible.

Acknowledgements

I would like to thank my wife for her gentle reminders that I could indeed complete this project. I would also like to thank Shirley Cooper and Leslie Hudson, without whom this book would be chock full of grammatical errors. Any errors still present are 100% my own doing. Special thanks to Anita Russell for the wonderful cover design. I would also like to thank John MacArthur and Danny Akin. Their commentary work on 1 John has been immensely valuable to me. Thank you First Baptist Church Dickson for allowing me to pursue an independent writing project and publish my own work.

CONTENTS

Introduction

In the fall of 2017, my pastor encouraged me to take what he called a "day with God". He asked me, along with other pastors on staff at the church where I work, to spend a whole day with nothing but our Bibles and a note pad. I live in middle Tennessee in a small town called Dickson just west of Nashville. When tasked with spending a whole day with just my Bible and a note pad, I immediately decided to go to Montgomery Bell State Park. I hike there often. I know the trails very well, and there are a few places with shelters where you can stop along the trails. My plan that morning was to pack my CamelBak™ pack with the essentials for spending the whole day out in the woods at the park.

There is also an old Cumberland Presbyterian Church on the park property near the trailhead. It is more of a historical site now, but groups still use it sometimes on Sundays to host services. But this was a week day, and the church was empty. Before hitting the trails, I decided to stop and sit in the church for a while. I began with a brief prayer asking God to direct me to where in His Word He wanted me to focus that day. Almost immediately I landed on the letter of 1 John. It's an oft-neglected letter tucked away in the back of the New Testament, but something drew me to it that morning.

Of course, I had read the letter before, but I had never dived deep into it. I had never expositionally broken it down verse by verse. I had never tackled its many themes and truths one by one. I intended to only read a few verses before departing on my hike that morning, but instead I found myself engrossed in the contents. I read the whole letter, not just once but twice, while sitting there that morning. God moved me by its simple, but extremely deep, truths. The rich content of the letter poured into my heart and did a number on me that day. It changed me. It broke me. It stirred my affections, engaged my intellect, and touched my spirit. I am a full-time vocational minister. It's my job, and blessing, to do ministry daily. But that morning God did ministry on me. I knew then and there I was supposed to do something with that small-yet-powerful letter, but I didn't know quite what it was.

When I first started to study in-depth this first letter of the Apostle John, I didn't expect to write a book about it. I was led to teach 1 John to a small group of about twenty people that I was meeting with once a month. That group started strong, but it eventually dwindled to around ten people. Most of those ten were there because they had to help me with the music, PowerPoint, and sound board. After six lessons, I concluded the meetings. I felt disheartened. I strongly felt God had led me to study this letter. I really believe He wanted me to share it with others. I was probably also over-confident in my own teaching ability and charisma.

Nonetheless, the desire to study this letter and to share its contents with others never lessened in my heart. I think the contents of this singular letter from the Apostle John has the ability to be earth-shaking and life-altering. I know it has been for me as I have studied it. I know many more could have, and indeed have, written a better book. I am no Greek scholar or expert at hermeneutics, but what lies before you as the reader is the culmination of two years of work. It was a long, hard journey for me, but it was a blessing.

My goal for this book is for it to be an encouragement and a practical guide for everyday believers. Although academic and scholarly people may enjoy the content and find it useful, my truest hope is that this book finds its way into the hands of laymen, laywomen, Sunday school teachers, disciples, evangelists, and missionaries. In other words, I hope everyone can find it helpful in some way.

But I also hope some may use this book as a tool that they can sit down with an unbelieving friend or family member and lead them to Christ. I hope this book can be used by a mature believer to disciple a new believer. I hope this book can be used by a missionary as they seek to teach foundational Christian truths to a new convert.

Maybe it goes without saying, but because this is a book about 1 John, it will be extremely helpful if you read the passage associated with the chapter before reading the chapter in this book. All of my interpretations and arguments point back to the text. So, by all means, spend some time reading the text from the Bible *before* reading my words about that text.

It was a blessing beyond compare to write the content of this book. I hope the Lord uses it to open the eyes of believers and unbelievers alike. To God be the glory for any kingdom building that results from this work.

"We are writing these things so that our joy may be complete" – 1 John 1:4

Chapter 1| Cherish Christ, the Word Made Flesh
1 John 1:1-4

I. Know Christ, the Word Made Flesh (v.1-2)

    a. His Deity

    b. His Humanity

II. Share Christ, the Word Made Flesh (v.3)

III. Find Joy in Christ, the Word Made Flesh (v.4)

Who is Jesus? That's a question all of us at some point have wrestled with. The people of Jesus' day wrestled with that question too, so much so that Jesus turned to his disciples one day and asked them, "...who do people say that I am?" (Mark 8:27) In Jesus' day, that question had several answers: prophet, teacher, Elijah, John the Baptist, etc. Jesus then made it personal when he asked his disciples, "but who do you say that I am?" (Mark 8:29) Peter, speaking for the rest, answered truthfully that Jesus was the Christ, the Son of God.

I remember when I began to debate in my own heart who Jesus is. I was thirteen years old and in the seventh grade. I had only been in church for a couple years at that point. In that moment, God began dealing with my heart, and the summer after my seventh grade year, I trusted Christ and placed my faith in Him. I began a life-long journey of following Him.

Asking the question "Who is Jesus?" is a life-changing question. How you respond to that question has eternal ramifications. Jesus either is who he claims to be, or He isn't. As C.S. Lewis put it in his book *Mere Christianity*:

"You must make your choice. Either this man was, and is, the Son of God: or else a madman or something worse. You can shut him up for a fool, you can spit at him and kill him as a demon; or you can fall at his feet and call him Lord and God. But let us not come with any patronizing nonsense about his being a great human teacher. He has not left that open to us. He did not intend to."[1]

No one knew better than the Apostle John who Jesus was. He made it His life's mission to tell people that Jesus was the Christ, the Son of God, and that by believing in Him you might have life in His name.

John wrote this letter to churches who were struggling. False teaching about the person of Jesus was causing division among believers and many were leaving the church. It is no wonder that he begins his letter with a bold affirmation of who Jesus is.

Many in today's world are still confused about the person of Jesus. These really are uncertain times we live in. But there is one thing we can be certain about, and that is that Jesus is who He said He was. God in His matchless grace has made it possible for us to know Jesus, He has commanded us to share Jesus with others, and He has called us to find all our joy in Jesus. Let's further explore these concepts below.

Know Christ, the Word Made Flesh (1:1-2)

---

[1] C.S. Lewis. *Mere Christianity* (San Francisco, CA: Harper San Francisco, 2001), 52

The first test of fellowship among believers is what they affirm about Christ. Christianity either stands or falls based on what we believe and teach about Jesus.

What John is affirming here is something that is so vital to Christianity. It is something we celebrate every year at Christmas. It is the incarnation of God. God himself became flesh in the person of Jesus Christ, the Eternal Son and second member of the Trinity. Right from the beginning of this letter John is affirming two very important things about Jesus.

His Deity:

John is affirming, "what was from the beginning". Christ has always existed along with God the Father. This is exactly how John began his Gospel, "In the beginning was the word...and the word was God...and dwelt [tabernacled] among us," (John 1:1; 14).

John's gospel also includes numerous "I am" statements from Jesus. In these, Jesus declares himself one with the Father.

- John 6:35, "I am the bread of life..."
- John 8:12, "...I am the Light of the world.."
- John 10:7, "I assure you, I am the door of the sheep"
- John 10:11, "I am the Good Shepherd..."
- John 11:25, "I am the resurrection and the life..."
- John 14:6, "I am the way, the truth, and the life..."
- John 15:1, "I am the true vine..."

In all of these passages, Jesus is declaring to us that He is for us what only God can be for us. He puts himself in the place of God. He is our bread, our provider, and our sustainer. He alone is the light in a dark world. He is the resurrection, and only in Him can the dead find life again. He encompasses everything that is true. By preceding all of these statements with the phrase "I am," all of his Jewish listeners would have known exactly what Jesus was doing: Jesus was declaring equality with God. That is why many were so appalled and troubled by these statements.

Jesus teaches this in other passages too. John 10:30 says, "I and the Father are one." Again in John 8:58, Jesus says, "Before Abraham was, I am." All of these passages, along with so many more, are ultimately why the Pharisees sought to kill Jesus. Here in the beginning of 1 John, the apostle is doing the same thing. He is declaring that Christ has been from the beginning. There never has been a time when the Son, Jesus, was not. He is God, and as such, He is eternal.

His Humanity:

John says about Jesus that he was "seen...observed...touched." Jesus was a tangible, flesh and blood human being. They saw Him with their eyes. They observed His movements and His actions. They touched Him, embraced Him, and walked with Him. They heard His words.

We may sometimes have a hard time thinking of Jesus in human terms. We wrestle with the concept of His humanity. Do we imagine how Jesus sounded when He sang? Do we picture Him chasing children, tickling them, and laughing hysterically as they wrestled Him to the ground? What was it like to be embraced by Jesus? He ate, drank, and slept. He mourned,

He wept, and He suffered. He got sick, He got angry, and He loved like no other human ever has.

This letter was written in the 90's AD. It is assumed John was also in his nineties at this time. That means sixty years had passed since Jesus had ascended, and John still remembered vividly and fondly his encounter and relationship with Jesus. John was one of the closest disciples and friends of Jesus. He saw the works of Jesus and heard his words more than most of the other twelve outside of Peter and James.

This strongly affirms John's account and his credibility with the churches. He was there when Christ was performing miracles. He was there when Lazarus was raised from his grave. He was there when Jesus was crucified, and he was the first to the empty tomb on resurrection morning. He had watched all his closest friends die as martyrs for their testimony about Christ.

John was not just a preacher of the Word; he intimately knew the Word. The gospel was not just a formula to a better life for him; it was eternal life itself.

To know Christ, to John, was not just head knowledge. He LOVED Jesus. Because of this, he can't help but "testify and declare" to others the word he has seen, touched, and heard. Jesus was not just a myth or a fable but the flesh and blood Son of God. He was God incarnate. John knew that only a fully-human and fully-God Jesus can grant eternal life. And only a fully-human and fully-divine Jesus could shed his blood as atonement for our sins. Only Jesus could defeat death and the grave. And that same Jesus is still ruling and reigning even now, and He will return in glory and power to judge the world.

Is it love for that portrait of Jesus that consumes us when we worship? Is it His word we are committed to living our lives by and dying for if need be? Is it His gospel, the good news, we are committed to sharing with others? Is it His love with which we are committed to loving each other?

The world has always been at odds with the concept of the incarnation, but to John it was vitally important.

Why is the incarnation a stumbling block to the world? John Piper said it this way in a sermon entitled *Eternal Life Has Appeared in Christ*:

> "…when God becomes a man, he strips away every pretense of man to be God. We can no longer do our own thing; we must do what this one Jewish man (Jesus) wants us to do. We can no longer pose as self-sufficient, because this one Jewish man says we are all sick with sin and must come to him for healing." [2]

As believers, it should be our desire to know Jesus more every day. To do that, we give ourselves to the study and mediation of his word. As our desire for Christ grows, so should our desire to share Christ.

Share Christ, the Word Made Flesh (1:3)

It is hard to articulate, I'm sure, the impact Jesus had on His disciples. Evangelism has turned into such a Christian buzzword. We have

---

[2] John Piper, "Eternal Life Has Appeared in Christ," Desiring God, Accessed January 23, 2020, https://www.desiringgod.org/messages/eternal-life-has-appeared-in-christ

made it simply a church program and turned it into a formula. We have tried to fit it into its own little box. Go door to door, hand out this pamphlet, or memorize this acrostic. Evangelism was not just a strategy or a program or a once-a-week visitation to the disciples; it was their life-blood. It was the air they breathed. What they had seen and heard was too amazing to keep to themselves. They shared about Jesus everywhere they went.

Their desire was to see others have fellowship along with them (v.3). They wanted others to experience the radical grace and salvation they had. They wanted others to hear the words of Jesus, the Messiah, and to experience the power of His Spirit in them the way He was in them.

To them, it was a sin to remain silent about this good news. Their love for Jesus overflowed into love for others.

John here uses the Greek word for fellowship, *koinonia*. Defined, this word means "sharing in common something that is significant or important." We often undervalue fellowship. To us, it often means meals or events and gatherings. To John, it was much more than that. Being together was important, but being in fellowship spiritually was much more. The vital thing that held their fellowship together, the most significant thing they held in common, was the gospel.

Gatherings and activities are great, but true fellowship is gospel-centered. If we as a church are not fellowshipping together by sharing the gospel, then our fellowship is lacking the key ingredient that truly makes it a fellowship. We cannot tell those around us every day that we love them if we do not share Jesus with them. If we love Jesus and we love people like Jesus, we should be sharing Jesus with them.

John knew that to invite others into the fellowship of the church was much more than that: inviting people to trust Christ was inviting them to be a part of something much bigger than themselves. It was inviting them into fellowship with God the Father, Christ the Son, and the Holy Spirit. When we share Jesus with others, we are inviting them to be a part of the local and universal church, the *eklessia*, the assembly of the One True God. We are inviting them to be part of the family of God.

I am sure this message was as appealing to those in John's day as it is now. Are you fatherless? God is a wonderful father. Do you have no family? We will be your brothers and sisters. For many in John's day, following Christ may have made them outcasts to their family. But in trusting Jesus, they gained a new family. If we allow Christ to work in us in our fellowship, a strong bond will be formed that can withstand anything. That is true fellowship, and it is an eternal fellowship.

Hans and Sophie Scholl understood the nature of true, eternal Christian fellowship. They were a brother and sister who were students in Munich, Germany, during the rise of the Third Reich. Initially, they were supporters of the Third Reich, but by the time the second World War was in full swing, they had gone from supporters to resistors. As students at the University of Munich, they helped form the student-led resistance movement named the *White Rose*.

They first began by creating leaflets with anti-Nazi messages in them meant to reveal truth and inspire resistance. They recognized that they were living in a time when many in Germany were closing their eyes to the atrocities committed by the Nazi regime. They also understood that what they were doing was considered high treason and punishable by death.

A second series of leaflets appeared highlighting the mass deportation and killing of Jews. They would mail these leaflets out, leave them in phone booths, or disperse them secretly in public places all over Munich.

The Scholls were raised Lutheran. Their Christian convictions led them to take a stand against the injustices of the Nazi regime. They often quoted Scripture and prominent Christian thinkers in their leaflets. Hans was quoted as saying, "It's high time that Christians made up their minds to do something...what are we going to show in the way of resistance...when all this terror is over? We will be standing empty-handed. We will have no answer when we are asked: 'What did you do about it?'"

Hans and Sophie eventually were spotted distributing leaflets and turned over to Nazi authorities. They confessed and took full responsibility for the actions of the *White Rose* organization. On February 22, 1943, they were taken before the German People's Court and declared guilty of high treason. They were beheaded later that day in Stadelheim Prison. Sophie was quoted as saying in her execution chamber, "God, you are my refuge into eternity". Hans declared in his cell, "Long live freedom!"

The Scholls realized, like many in the Apostle John's day, that in Christ they had found a new community, a greater community. They had found an eternal community. They were willing to sacrifice themselves for a cause in order to display Christ to a lost and dying world.[3]

Many of the greatest Christian movements of the last 500 years were started by young adults who had a deep love and passion for Christ and His word. They were willing to stand against the tide of culture and proclaim the gospel (all of it) even if it cost their lives.

---

[3] Sara Barratt, "75 Years Ago Today: The Incredible Story of Hans and Sophie Scholl," The Gospel Coalition, Published on February, 22, 2018, https://www.thegospelcoalition.org/article/75-years-ago-hans-sophie-scholl/.

The resistance movement that included the Scholls was student led. Students didn't join it because it was a popular program, but because it was an earth-shaking and life-changing movement.

Don't think you've got to do something spectacular to change the world. Embrace the gospel, even when it's not popular, and let Christ use you to be part of his world-changing work. When you do this, it will lead to a deep, abiding joy in your heart.

Find Joy in Christ, the Word Made Flesh (1:4)

A product of knowing Christ and living a life of sharing Christ is joy. It is a fruit of the Spirit. God produces true joy in us. Joy is also the purpose of John's letter.

He says in verse four, "We are writing these things so that our joy may be complete." His purpose is for the churches to experience joy because of the truth contained in his letter. The phrase "these things" is primarily referring to a shared fellowship with Jesus the Son and God the Father that produces joy in our lives. God is glorified in His people when they find their joy in Him. John's joy was in knowing Christ, in sharing Him with others, and in seeing believers grow in their knowledge of Christ.

What does the Bible say about joy? It speaks loudly to what true joy is and what it is centered upon.

First, it is a gift from God. Galatians 5:22 says, "But the fruit of the Spirit is ...joy." True joy is something that arises from a heart that has been transformed and changed by the Holy Spirit. We cannot experience joy in its truest sense without being born again.

Secondly, it is not based on current circumstances but on God's promises. Joy is rooted in the truth of who God is and what He has done for us in Christ Jesus. To know Christ is to find lasting joy in Him and Him alone. It is to lean on His promises and find all our hope in them. He is the source of all joy.

Third, the Bible speaks of joy in relation to suffering and tribulation. James 1:2-4 says, "Consider it great joy my brothers, whenever you experience various trials knowing that the testing of your faith produces endurance but endurance must do its complete work, so that you may be mature and complete, lacking nothing." Another way of saying this is that our joy in the midst of suffering is made possible because of Christ's suffering for us. One author of a *Table Talk* devotional puts it this way:

"We are to consider what we are going through as a matter of joy, not because the thing itself is something that is pleasurable, but because tribulation works patience within us. There is at least one good thing happening to us in the midst of pain and suffering. We are therefore called to think about our circumstances in that light. Our suffering is not an exercise in futility. God has a purpose, and that purpose is always good. We can count all things **joy** because God is working in all situations, even the most painful, for our sanctification and ultimate glorification."[4]

The last thing I would say of the nature of joy is that it is centered on Christ's joy in us. Hebrews 12:1-2 says, "...let us lay aside every weight

---

[4] "Counting It All Joy", Ligonier, Accessed on January 22, 2020, https://www.ligonier.org/learn/devotionals/counting-it-all-joy-2/.

and sin that so easily ensnares us. Let us run with endurance the race that lies before us, keeping our eyes on Jesus, the source and perfecter of our faith who for the joy laid before Him endured a cross and despised the shame and has sat down at the right hand of God's Throne." Christ endured a despised cross for the sake of His Bride, the Church. He looked ahead and saw the joy that our redemption would bring to His Father and to Him. Because of that joy fueling him and sustaining him, he was able to face and endure the horror of the cross. What a life-giving and sanctifying thing joy can be in the life of a believer!

This joy isn't a partial joy either. God desires for our joy to be complete. This means to make full. It is an all you could ever want or need kind of joy. It is a fulfilling joy and a "no matter what happens, I can still rejoice" kind of joy. In Christ, this type of joy is possible.

Is your joy lacking? Is it not full or complete? Are you abiding in Christ? Are you fully experiencing fellowship with Jesus and God the Father? Are you sharing Jesus with others? Are you in fellowship with other followers of Jesus? All of these things influence our joy.

We often undervalue the importance of joy. We often treat joy and happiness as circumstantial and as if they are emotions not to be trusted. However, if true joy is lacking in our lives, then it could mean that something serious spiritually is out of balance. It means something is missing in our lives. Are you finding your joy complete by trusting in and sharing Jesus, the true Word of God?

We should commit our lives to knowing Christ the Word. We should commit to sharing Jesus, the Word. And we should endeavor to find all our joy in Jesus, the Word. Do you know Jesus today? Have you trusted Him to forgive your sins and save you from the wrath of God? Jesus, the Word made flesh, stands ready to save.

Christian, have you been sharing Jesus with others? Do you need to re-commit to telling the world about Jesus? Jesus, the Word made flesh, is immensely valuable, and He is worth sharing.

Is your joy lacking? Is there something keeping your joy from being full and complete? Jesus, the Word made flesh, stands wiling to complete your joy. In a confusing and uncertain world, learning to cherish Christ and finding all our joy in Him can make all the difference.

Chapter 2| Confronting The Problem of Sin
John 1:5-2:2

I.   Confronting Sin Means Exposing It to God's Light (v.5)

II.   Confronting Sin Means Walking in the Light (v.6-10)

III.   Confronting Sin Means Placing All Our Hope And Trust in Christ Alone (2:1-2)

Why do we need a Savior? We often talk about the saving power of Jesus, but do we ever pause and think about what is it about us that needs saving? What is wrong with us and why do we need to be rescued? The simple answer to that is sin, but in reality it's more complicated. The nature of sin goes all the way back to the garden of Eden to the first man and first woman. In choosing to disobey God, they set mankind on a course of living underneath the curse of sin and death. Death, after all, is the just, deserved wage of sin (Romans 6:23). See, death is actually unnatural to the human condition as it was meant to be. Death was not an experience man was originally intended to have. We weren't meant to experience the pain and suffering and the profound sense of loss that comes with death. We often associate sin and death as just part of humanity, but that is not how the Bible defines humanity. Humanity was supposed to live in perfect harmony with God, in constant fellowship with Him, taking delight in Him and all He provided, and enjoying and cultivating the perfect world He had made. Sin destroyed that. Therefore, sin and death are actually an invasion into the human experience as God intended it. That is why if we are going to understand God's unfailing love for His people, we must understand the sin issue in the heart of every human that makes the times we live in so uncertain.

We must stop seeing sin as just an act or a series of acts and start seeing it also as a condition of our hearts. It is from that condition we need to be rescued, and from which we must be saved if we are to be restored in fellowship with a perfect and holy God. Wayne Grudem defines sin as "any failure to conform to the moral law of God in act, attitude, or nature."[1] John Piper says sin is, "any feeling or thought or action that comes from a heart that does not treasure God above all things."[2] Acts of sin flow from a heart diseased with sin. Sin is something we must all face, and we must all deal with it. We must teach our kids about sin, and we desperately need rescuing from sin. The greatest threat to our kids or is not the world; it is the sin inside each of us. If we are to be people made right with God, sin must be dealt with. But how do you talk about sin in a culture of moral relativism? Moral relativism is the doctrine that knowledge, truth, and morality exist in relation to culture, society, or historical context. In other words, what is considered to be right or wrong is not a fixed absolute but rather relative to the tide of culture. So individuals, society, and the current culture get to dictate what moral values they hold to or reject. Moral

---

[1] Wayne Grudem. *Systematic Theology: An Introduction to Biblical Doctrine* (Grand Rapids, MI: Zondervan, 2000), 490
[2] John Piper, "Sin Prefers Anything to God," Desiring God, Published April 8, 2015, https://www.desiringgod.org/interviews/sin-prefers-anything-to-god

relativism rejects the notion of an absolute standard of morality that all must abide by or follow.

John deals with just that in this passage. John had to teach the truth about sin in a culture were sin wasn't taken very seriously. In this passage, John talks of the nature of sin as well as the remedy for sin. I hope this will help us all see the destructive nature of sin, confront sin in our own lives, and prompt us to teach our kids about it. I also hope for us to see what lengths God has gone to make sure sin doesn't have the final say in our lives.

Confronting Sin Means Exposing It to God's Light (1:5)

More than anything, John desired to tell people the truth about God. He is convinced that the message that he has come from God. God has testified to us the truth about Himself and His Son, Jesus. We, like John, have good news that the world needs.

God is Light

We often see this comparison between light and dark in Scripture. Light is seen as something pure and often refers to truth or holiness. Darkness is the opposite of light. It represents sin and falsehood. The book of Psalms refers to God as "light and salvation," (Psalm 27:1). Isaiah says the "glory of the Lord shines," (Isaiah 60:1). John in his gospel calls Jesus "the true Light" and "the Light of the World," (John 1:9; 8:12).

Two truths about light that are also true of God is that light gives life, and light exposes what's in the dark. Isaiah 9:2 says, "People walking in darkness have seen a great Light; a light has dawned on those living in the land of darkness." God is light, and He is holy and good and pure. He is everything darkness is not, and by His light He drives out darkness. He gives life, and He exposes the dark places of our lives, the sin indwelling each of us.

John says in verse five that "there is absolutely no darkness in Him." In the Greek this is a double negative. I once heard someone say a double negative is bad grammar, but in the Bible, it is great theology. In the Greek, double negatives were used to strongly emphasize something. What is being strongly emphasized here is the perfection and holiness of God. Not even a single hint of a shadow of darkness is present in the nature of God.

God is sin's antithesis. The character of God is everything sin is not. He is its exact opposite, and He stands opposed to it. This is the starting point to understanding the destructive nature of sin. You can't possibly see how devastating the darkness of sin is until it is exposed to the holiness of the light of God.

Have you ever experienced utter darkness in a cavern or cave? How did that make you feel? Did you feel panicked as if the world was falling in on you? Did the darkness seem to have a tangible weight that seemed heavy on you? How uneasy did it make you feel to not know what was around you or to be able to see where your next step would be? How comforting was it when the light was finally turned on?

Sin is even more devastating that true darkness, and that's what John discusses next.

Confronting Sin Means Walking in the Light (1:6-10)

Be Honest with Others About Sin (v.6-7)

The false teachers of John's day claimed to have fellowship with Christ, with the Light, yet they walked in darkness. In other words, they claimed to be walking in the light but lived a lifestyle of open sin. Their words and actions did not match. The Gnostics of John's day saw everything material as evil and only the spiritual was good. So sin committed in the flesh wasn't really sin. They taught that you could do whatever you wanted in the flesh because it was evil and would perish.

They were deceiving other people about their own sin. They downplayed the seriousness of sin. We see that in our culture, as well, because we often allow culture to dictate what is good or bad, sin or not. Again, the Bible speaks of sin as a condition of our heart that leads to a lifestyle of disobedience to God. Those who walk in the light are honest with others about their sin. John says in verse six that the truth must be practiced-- not just talked about. To claim the truths about Christ and then to live a lifestyle out of sync with those truths is to lie about who we are and who Christ is.

To "walk in the light" (v.7) means to develop a continuous and consistent pattern of life that believes what Jesus taught about Himself and to live out those truths daily. If we do this, two things happen. First, we have fellowship with each other (because we are not lying to each other about our sin). Secondly, Jesus cleanses us from sin. This is a beautiful truth. Walking in the light doesn't mean you won't stumble and sin. It means you will recognize sin for what it is and continually run to Christ for forgiveness. This cleansing that is referred to in this verse is a continual cleansing. This means that every day Christ is removing the stain of sin from your life. We'll understand more about this soon, but it is awesome to know that every day Jesus stands with you in your battle with darkness and the flesh.

Be Honest with Yourself About Your Sin (v.8-9)

Again, moral relativism teaches us to lie to *ourselves* about sin. "You are fine the way you are." "If it is right to you then it's right, so don't believe what everybody else says." "Live your truth."

We confront these lies by reminding ourselves daily about who we are. 1 John 2:8 says that we deceive ourselves when we aren't honest about what sin is. Moral relativism is dangerous because it teaches us to lie to ourselves every day. If sin is relative, then it becomes easy to justify anything and everything you say and do. Don't lie to yourself!

Those who walk in the light are honest with themselves about their sin. When we acknowledge sin in our lives, then we acknowledge our reliance on the Savior. As Christians, our lives aren't defined by sin any longer, but that doesn't mean sin won't happen. Genuine believers admit sin and repent or turn from it. You serve a God who stands ready to forgive. Christ stands as one who is both "faithful and righteous" (v.9) to forgive. John will soon point out that we can't fix our sin issue; only Christ can.

Be Honest About What God Says About Your Sin (v.10)

Those who walk in the light are honest about what God says about their sin. God has emphatically described mankind's condition as having the stain of sin:

- Psalm 14:3, "All have turned away; all alike have become corrupt. There is no one who does good, not even one."

- Isaiah 53:6, "We all went astray like sheep; we all have turned to our own way; and the Lord has punished Him for the iniquity of us all."

- Jeremiah 17:9, "The heart is more deceitful than anything else, and incurable-who can understand it?"

- Romans 3:23, "For all have sinned and fall short of the glory of God."

God has declared two things about us we best not ignore: one, we are great sinners; two, we are in desperate need of a Savior. John says, rather bluntly, that those who would claim to be without sin do not have God's word in them. In other words, they have no fellowship with God.

We dare not call God a liar nor dismiss sin as relative. It's important we remember these truths as we seek to teach our children about the reality of sin. Our children, like us, are born sinners into a world cursed by sin. You don't have to teach a child how to sin; it's in their nature. As they grow older, we must be honest with them about sin. One of the most important questions my mother ever asked me was "Do you believe you have no sin?" In our house, we call sins bad choices. We teach our children that we make bad choices because of a sin problem in our heart. Because we all have a sinful heart and make bad choices, we need forgiveness. We teach them that Jesus died so our heart could be changed and we could be forgiven of our bad choices. Our children will see no need for a Savior if they aren't at some point crushed by the reality of their sin.

See, walking in the light confronts sin in our lives because walking in the light reminds us of who we were when Christ rescued us. It also reminds us of who we are now: believers in the midst of being remade by the power of Christ. It assures us of who He is making us to be: His perfected children that will dwell with Him forever in His kingdom. John next turns to two great truths about Jesus that provide the remedy for sin.

Confronting Sin Means Placing All Our Hope and Trust in Christ Alone (2:1-2)

Christ, Our Advocate

Notice how John refers to the people in 2:1 as "my little children." John is an old man by this time. He has deep, fatherly affection for these people. He is grieved that they have been led astray by false teaching. He is grieved that some have abandoned the church altogether to follow people who would lead them deeper into the darkness of sin. He has one desire for His people: "that you may not sin."

In a culture that dismissed the reality of sin, John was telling his people to turn away from it. Sin does still happen in the life of a believer, but we are not powerless over it. God has put His Spirit in us, and He has made Christ our Advocate.

What does Advocate mean? In the Greek, it is the word *parakletos*. It means to be called to one's side. It pictures someone who pleads the cause of someone else before a judge. It is someone who acts as legal counsel. Some translations use the word "helper" here.

The picture is of Christ as a defense attorney. Revelation 12:10 says of Satan that he "is an accuser of our brothers and sisters, who accuses them before God day and night." Christian, Christ is your legal defense before this accuser at the judgment seat of God. Jesus is a very good attorney because, unlike an earthly defense attorney, he can guarantee your acquittal. See, in Christ, the guilty can stand before God and be declared innocent. So confronting sin means reminding yourself daily that Christ is in your corner doing battle for you.

This is why the doctrine of moral relativism is so dangerous. It tells you that you make the rules. You declare right from wrong, and you live according to the values you set as good. In essence, relativism makes you God. It makes you your own defense attorney. In the world of relativism, you become judge and jury, and you represent yourself.

So here is a very important question: can you represent yourself before a holy and just God? What defense could you possibly offer for yourself that would be good enough to acquit you? The answer has to be "nothing." It's why we need Christ as our Advocate. He can defend us because of this next truth from 1 John 2:2.

Christ, Our Propitiation

Christ can be our Advocate because he is also our propitiation or atonement. This is a radical truth. The Greek word translated here as atonement or propitiation is *hilasmos*. It simply means to appease or satisfy. A similar Greek word is used in Romans 3:25 when it talks of God "setting forth" Christ as a propitiation. So what did the death of Christ satisfy, and why does that matter for us?

It satisfied God's wrath and punishment for our sins. It's important for us to understand that a very real transaction took place on the cross. The cross isn't just a symbol of sacrifice. It is the fulfillment of God's just penalty for sin. Paul puts it this way in Colossians 2:14, "He erased the certificate of debt, with its obligations, that was against us and opposed to us, and has taken it out of the way by nailing it to the cross." The certificate of debt mentioned is our debt of sin.

Because of our sin, we deserved punishment. We could never, on our own, satisfy the righteous requirements of a holy God. We could never erase that debt. But Christ took it upon himself on the Cross. He took *our* punishment. He took *our* pain. He experienced the wrath of God on *our* behalf. He atoned for *our* sin. Christ was crucified so that we might, by placing our faith in him, be reconciled to God.

When, in John 19:30, Christ on the cross said "It is finished," that's what He meant. He paid in full what we owed God because of our sin. Christ, The Righteous One, was hung on a cross in place of sinners. The cross is where the wrath of God and the mercy of God meet. Christian, He is your atonement in every sense of the word. He stood accused in our place. Our advocate and our defender became our curse and propitiation.

I have so much more I could say here, but I think Paul sums it up best when he says in Romans 5:8, "God proves his love for us in that while we were still sinners, Christ died for us."

In a world where sin isn't taken seriously, we look to the cross and it says otherwise. We belittle the cross when we fail to see sin for what it is. The cross tells us everything we need to know about sin and about ourselves. The truth of Christ as propitiation, when I first truly understood it, broke me. The death of Christ wasn't the result of a world gone mad, but it was the result of my sin meeting God's love. In order to reconcile me, Christ had to be crushed. Do we mourn that? Do we rejoice in that?

The beautiful thing is that for those who have trusted Christ, sin no longer has power over you. Christ has set you free, not just from the deserved punishment for sin, but from its power here and now and for forever.

The third verse of a newer hymn, *Come Behold the Wondrous Mystery*, sums this concept up very well:

> "Come behold the wondrous mystery
> Christ the Lord upon the tree
> In the stead of ruined sinners
> Hangs the Lamb in victory
> See the price of our redemption
> See the Father's plan unfold
> Bringing many sons to glory
> Grace unmeasured, love untold"[3]

So how do you confront sin in a culture of moral relativism? You shine a light on it, you walk in the light, and you run to and embrace the cross. Sin and death are very real, but they hold no power over those in Christ because He has defeated both.

If you have never trusted Christ, if you have never turned from your sin and placed all your hope in Him, I encourage you to run to Him right now. Do it in your heart now wherever you are. Tell someone about that decision.

If you are like me, and the truth of Christ as advocate and atonement has hit you hard right now like never before, just take some time and thank Him. Praise Him for the cross.

---

[3] Matt Papa, Matt Boswell, and Michael Bleecker, "Come Behold the Wondrous Mystery, " in *Hymns of Grace* (Los Angeles: The Master's Seminary Press, 2015), 184

There might be someone reading this that is trapped by a certain sin. Over and over it keeps coming back. Remember, in Christ, sin has no power over you. Run to Him. Give it to Him. He's already paid the price for it.

Chapter 3| Embracing Radical Love
1 John 2:3-17

When we hear the word *obedience*, it often brings up negative images, especially when we apply that to Christianity. To say that God desires our obedience often brings to mind trying to please God by doing good deeds. We think of the ungodly Pharisees and scribes of Jesus' day burdening people with laws and man-made traditions in order to earn God's favor. A wrong view of obedience might lead us to thinking that if we could only do the right things, God would be pleased with us. If we were only religious enough, God would accept us.

Early on in my Christian walk, I felt that God was accepting me because I had done and said all the right things. I was practicing obedience the way I had been taught. I went to church. I sang in the choir, and I did not listen to popular contemporary Christian music (because I was taught that was bad and hymns and southern gospel were good, although country music was completely fine). I dressed as I was supposed to and did not cuss most of the time. I was convinced that if I were to stop doing those things, I would be backsliding and God would eventually let me slip back into lostness. I was often proud in my obedience. I was more like the Pharisee than the tax collector in Jesus' parable in Luke 18. I might not have said it out loud, but in my heart I prayed like the Pharisee. In my prayer life, I pointed towards my works, my faithfulness to the church, and to what I considered to be the right view of things. I thought that these actions and thoughts gave me a closer standing with God. In reality, I should have been praying more like the sinful tax collector. Luke said that he "would not even raise his eyes to heaven but kept striking his chest and saying, 'God, have mercy on me, a sinner!' I tell you, this one went down to his house justified rather than the other; because everyone who exalts himself will be humbled, but the one who humbles himself will be exalted," (Luke 18:13-14).

My obedience was fueled by the fact that if I did all the right stuff, if I was being a good Christian, and God was happy with me, He might not send me to hell. God had to break me of that mindset. He brought me to a place where I was more like the publican. I still have moments of pride, but in the midst of those moments God sends me reminders (a lot of times through my wife) that I'm still that publican on my knees striking my chest in desperate need of God's mercy.

That is the heart of obedience. It is a heart that treasures Christ above all things and realizes we are nothing apart from the work of Jesus on the cross. Obedience can be defined as the overflow of love and joy in who Christ is and what He has done. It is right actions that flow from a heart completely satisfied in, and in awe of, the glory of God.

That is how John approaches obedience here. For John, love and obedience are eternally and inseparably connected in Scripture. Jesus says in John 14:15, "if you love me you will keep my commands." That is something John addresses in this letter. If someone claims to love God but does not do what he says, then he is a liar. He reminds his readers that obedience to God is made possible by the fact that Christ has died as propitiation for our sins. Therefore, you are freed to obey God. Because we are in Him and He is in us, He empowers us to live a life of love for God that leads to obedience. These were his reasons for writing: to remind them of who they were and of the victory they had over sin.

Spirit Empowered Obedience (2:3-6)

1 John 2:3 says, "This is how we have come to know…" John, before diving into the topic of obedience being the display of our love for God, points back to the work of Christ as advocate and propitiation or atonement. You cannot obey God if you have not experienced the atonement of Christ for your sins, and without him being a constant advocate for you before God.

We have been radically saved by Christ, and this leads to radical obedience for Christ. John says that to know God, through Christ, is to obey him. Obedience is the overflow of joy that you have been saved by Christ and spared the wrath of God through his atoning death on the cross.

Belief and obedience go hand-in-hand. Knowing, loving, and obeying God are all interconnected. One will always lead to the others. In knowing and loving God, He enables us by His Spirit to obey.

John says that to claim to know God, but to have no fruit of obedience or no love for the things or commands of Christ, is to be a liar. Something that should be said of the people of God is that they obey God. This is a test of our fellowship. Are we encouraging each other to not only believe rightly but to live rightly? John MacArthur says it this way "Those genuinely born again display the habit of obedience."[1]

John says about those who keep God's word that the "...love of God is perfected in Him," and that those who remain in God and who follow Him, "...walk as Christ walked." So obedience is not just the proof of our love for God, it is also the assurance of our salvation. How do you know you are "in Him?" John says you walk as Jesus walked. And it is impossible to walk as Jesus walked unless you are "in Him" and He in you.

Jesus reiterates the same thing himself in John 15:1-8:

"I am the true vine, and my Father is the gardener. [2] Every branch in me that does not produce fruit he removes, and he prunes every branch that produces fruit so that it will produce more fruit. [3] You are already clean because of the word I have spoken to you. [4] Remain in me, and I in you. Just as a branch is unable to produce fruit by itself unless it remains on the vine, neither can you unless you remain in me. [5] I am the vine; you are the branches. The one who remains in me and I in him produces much fruit, because you can do nothing without me. [6] If anyone does not remain in me, he is thrown aside like a branch and he withers. They gather them, throw them into the fire, and they are burned. [7] If you remain in me and my words remain in you, ask whatever you want and it will be done for you. [8] My Father is glorified by this: that you produce much fruit and prove to be my disciples."

---

[1] John MacArthur. *The MacArthur Bible Commentary* (Nashville, TN: Thomas Nelson, 2005), 1952

Those who seek to love God more will come to know Him more, and those who come to know Him more will love Him more. That is the heart of obedience. It is the result of knowing and treasuring who God is and what He did for us. For so long, I thought obedience was simply doing the right things and prided myself in that. I came to find out that obedience is about treasuring Christ so that He might grow a passion and affection in me to do what pleases God.

This leads to a spirit-empowered walk (life) that looks like Jesus' life. He is the pattern. He is the model. It is by abiding in Him and walking like Him that we can do both of the things John mentions next.

A Story of Two Loves

A Radical Love for Each Other (2:7-11)

John says in this passage, "I am not writing to you an old command but a new command." Most scholars believe that John wrote his letters after his gospel. Most scholars also assume that the churches that received the letters had knowledge of John's Gospel, especially in verses 7-11 where John seems to refer to his gospel account (John 13:34-35) that says, "I give you a new command: Love one another. Just as I have loved you, you are also to love one another. By this everyone will know that you are my disciples, if you love one another."

So the command to love one another has been there since the beginning of their Christian experience. As a matter of fact, the command is so old that it goes all the way back to Moses and the Law. Leviticus 19:17-18 says, "Do not harbor hatred against your brother. Rebuke your neighbor directly, and you will not incur guilt because of him. Do not take revenge or bear a grudge against members of your community, but love your neighbor as yourself; I am the LORD."

We are not just called to trust Christ, but in trusting him we are enabled to walk as He walked, which means that our affections are changed. We are transformed into loving people. The command to love was always there, but Jesus, as with most things, raised the standard of love. We are not only to love but to love as He loved. Jesus personified the love of God and by His Spirit has poured out that love on us. Romans 5:5 says, "God's love has been poured out in our hearts through the Holy Spirit who was given to us."

This type of love is a supernatural love only displayed by those who follow Him, who are drawn out of darkness into His light. John loved to talk about love. John 17:24-26 is one of the most beautiful passages in the Bible:

"Father, I want those you have given me to be with me where I am, so that they will see my glory, which you have given me because you loved me before the world's foundation. 25 Righteous Father, the world has not known you. However, I have known you, and they have known that you sent me. 26 I made your name known to them and will continue to make it known, so that the love you have loved me with may be in them and I may be in them."

That type of love, the love of Jesus in us, is even now dispelling darkness in our hearts. Those who display that they are still in darkness are obviously not in the light. One of the ways that this plays out is how you either love or hate your brother. The word "brother" in 2:9-10 is referring to fellow believers. Those who have no love for the church or for the people of God are not in the light. John leaves no gray area here.

Hatred, not love, was a mark of the false teachers of John's day. They lived a lifestyle marked by that hatred and thus led people into darkness and not into light. John said that those who love their brothers and sisters have no cause to stumble. They are in the light. They see clearly because of Christ.

John reminds his readers of how dangerous hatred is. He warns that those who have a pattern of life that is hateful toward others are "in darkness." (v.9) All throughout the Bible, darkness is a metaphor for spiritual death and lostness. Those who are in the dark walk (or live their life) in the dark. They do not know where they are going (directionless), and they are blind. Living in darkness means there is an absence of God, and therefore, an absence of love, from their life. The problem is that they, in their sin, have become accustomed to the dark.

It's clear that our obedience and love for God is displayed, and proved, by our love for each other, brothers and sisters in Christ. Remember, in 1 John 1:5 John said that Christ was "light and there is absolutely not darkness in Him." To be in Christ means to be in the light, and that leads to a supernatural and deep love for those for whom Christ died. It is a sacrificial love. That type of love comes at a cost. What are we denying ourselves or giving up in order to more fully love our brothers and sisters? If we as believers are going to navigate uncertain times, we must learn to sacrificially love our brothers and sisters in Christ. We must lean on them in difficult times. The church is to be a living display of the sacrificial love of Christ. When the church of Jesus loves this way, it is a beautiful display of the gospel to the world.

It took me a long time to fully understand the beautiful diversity of the church. The church is people from all backgrounds and walks of life fully devoted to each other and growing in a love that is not natural, nor man-made, but enabled by God. When you experience this kind of love, it leads you to reject another kind.

A Rejection of the Love of the World (2:15-17)

John spends v.12-14 reminding the people of who they are. He reminds them that they are children of God and children of the light. They have been forgiven in the name of Jesus, and they have come to know God. These truths in and of themselves are amazing. The God of the universe has made himself known in Christ and has shone a light on our dark hearts so that we might be called His children. What wonderful news!

Not only that, but because they have come to know God and have been forgiven, they are strong in Christ. Strong enough, in fact, that through His power they have victory over the evil one. This fulfills that old promise God made to Adam and Eve way back in Genesis 3:15, that He would one day send a Savior to crush the head of the serpent. In Christ, there is true victory over sin and death and Satan and every ounce of darkness in this world. The Snake-crusher, Christ, has defeated the Devil.

John wants this church to know these sacred truths. Don't be led astray by false teaching that leads to hatred. Embrace the one who gave you victory and who forgave you. That will enable you to love each other deeply and reject a love for this world.

I should take a moment and define the word "world" here. It is not referring to the material world or the people of the world. What is talked about here is a world system that rebels against and rejects the things of

God. MacArthur says it is an "invisible spiritual system of evil dominated by Satan."[2] It is a system that opposes God, His word, and His people. Anything that would seek to draw your love and affection away from God is included in this statement. We'll talk more about the specifics of this worldview in a moment.

Now back to the topic. Do not love the world or the things in it. Anything that would be contrary to God's word or anything that would draw our love (even just an ounce of it) away from God is to be rejected. The truth is that we all long for love, and we all give our love to something or someone. Coming to Christ means he reorders our affections. He gives us new loves. Experiencing the love of God and giving our love to Him is the fullness of Christian joy and satisfaction. God wants to bring you to a place where you can say, "You are all I need. I am satisfied in you and you alone, Lord. All of my love is devoted to you. You are my joy." This is the whole point. To give your love to anything else but the Love of your soul is, in the words of Danny Akin, President of Southeastern Seminary, to "give it to a lesser lover."[3] All true love, for our spouse, our kids, or each other, comes from devoting ourselves to and loving Christ as our Supreme Love.

In verse 16, John says that everything that belongs to the world is not of God. The world cannot give you what you long for, so we should reject it. He names three things here, three weapons so to speak, the world would use to draw away your affections from God.

First is the lust of the flesh. Desires in and of themselves are not bad or evil so to speak. The question we must ask is what is the object of our

---

[2] MacArthur, *The MacArthur Bible Commentary*, 1954
[3] Daniel L. Akin. *Christ-Centered Exposition: Exalting Jesus in 1, 2, and 3 John*, eds. David Platt, Daniel L. Akin, and Tony Merida (Nashville, TN: B&H Publishing Group, 2014), 40

desires? The temptation of the flesh and the lure of the world would drive us to seek to fulfill our desires in ways contrary to God's will and His word. This isn't just speaking of sexual immorality but any fleshly desire. This could be desire for affection, companionship, food, intellectual engagement, etc.

John is saying that in Christ you already have everything you need to have all these desires met. But because we still have indwelling sin, we must recognize that sometimes we are tempted to pursue things that aren't good for us, even when they seem good at first. So do not run to the world to have your desires met; run to the one who created you with those desires instead, and let Him fulfill them.

Next John deals with the lust of the eyes. This refers to what you see. Your eyes are a gateway to your mind and heart. David lusted for Bathsheba because he "saw" her bathing. Sometimes this world will use things that are attractive to draw our minds and hearts away from God. What you see has a profound effect on you. I'm sure all of us can picture something in our life we have seen and never been able to forget. Sight is a very powerful sense. It is after all what lured Eve to the forbidden fruit.

We should be careful what we let our eyes see. Focus your mind's eye on Christ. He is supremely beautiful. Don't allow your sight to draw you away to give in to sinful appetites. Many things that have a beautiful appearance can lead to death in the end.

Third is the pride of life or of one's lifestyle. This one is tricky, but I believe it is referring to being prideful or boastful about either what you have (possessions) or how you live. We are tempted to make an idol out of our possessions, our achievements, and our position.

The world is so tricky in how it labels things. It says "Be proud to be (you name it), a woman, a man, an American, a soldier, a teacher, etc." All of these things have merit. Of course, there are sinful things people often take pride in as well. This is just another way Satan takes something good and makes it an idol. Many of the things we are tempted to make idols out of are not in and of themselves bad. We need teachers, soldiers, faithful Americans, and men and women. But are they your boast? Are they where you get your sense of pride? Because there is only one thing Scripture says in which we should boast. Galatians 6:14 says, "But as for me, I will never boast about anything except the cross of our Lord Jesus Christ. The world has been crucified to me through the cross, and I to the world." What Paul is saying in this passage is that the world is spiritually counted as dead, of no use. In the same way, Paul has been crucified to the world. Meaning that he has also died to the things of the world.

Never allow God's good things to take the place of God. The cross is the source of all our blessings. The cross is where our victory was achieved. The ultimate reason, according to 1 John 2:17, to not give any of our affection to the world is because ultimately it will not last. The world, along with all its lusts, is passing away.

John reminds us to give all our hope, affection, and love to God. He is eternal and any investment made in Him will last forever. What good does it do us to have all the stuff the world desires for us to have, but to lose Christ along the way? For the sake of our eternal souls, we should devote all we have to the things that are eternal.

The Apostle Paul provides us an example in Demas of someone who lost sight of the eternal. He is mentioned by Paul in Colossians as a companion to Luke in the work of the gospel. There, he is commended by Paul, but Demas takes a turn for the worse somewhere along the way. By the time Paul writes 2 Timothy at the end of his life, knowing he will die soon, he says, "Demas has deserted me because he loved this present world," (2 Timothy 3:10). Demas serves as a warning and an example that some have and will lose sight of the eternal. If Demas, a man commended by an apostle and a companion to Luke in the work of the gospel, can lose sight, then so can we. Don't be like Demas. Give all you have here and now to the eternal work of the gospel.

I hope it is clear at this point that our obedience is rooted in our love for God. That love overflows into love for each other and a rejection of the love of the world. To put it another way, our obedience is an overflow of our joy and delight in God.

For so long, I thought obedience was doing the right things so God would be satisfied with me. But I have come to realize that obedience comes from a soul completely and utterly satisfied in Him, and from a heart that finds all its joy in Christ. I realize now that obedience does not earn me favor with God. Rather, it is a response of gratitude to the favor God has so undeservedly bestowed upon me. We should pray for eyes to see Him as supremely beautiful. So beautiful, in fact, that everything else in this world pales in comparison to Him.

I have a long way to go, and you do too. I hope that as we learn more about what it means to be satisfied in Christ that we will also learn more and more about what it means to love our brothers and sisters. I pray God would give us the strength to reject the love of the world that is so fleeting and passing away. Embrace the eternal. Embrace the walk Christ walked. Embrace the self-sacrificing, world-rejecting, eternal love of Christ. May that kind of love be found in you, and may that kind of radical love be shown to you.

Chapter 4| Abiding in Christ in an Anti-Christ Culture
1 John 2:18-27

The Lord created human beings with five senses: touch, taste, sight, smell, and hearing. He gave us those senses in order for us to fully experience and interact with the world He made for us. Our problem is that as fallen human beings, we often get wrapped up in the material world. We often obsess over the things we have or don't have. We get caught up in the things that appeal to these five senses. We get so wrapped up in these sensory experiences that it aggravates us and sometimes makes us depressed as we get older and these senses start to fade. The good news for us is that this world, which is also fading away, was never meant to be our permanent reality.

The Bible is clear that there is a supernatural world. It is a dimension we cannot perceive with our physical senses, but it is nonetheless very real and very active. This includes heaven, hell, angels, and demons. We don't often spend a lot of time in our churches talking about angels or demons or the Devil, but they are very real. However, I do believe an over-fascination with the demonic aspect of this supernatural world can be unhealthy, but so is completely ignoring it. C.S. Lewis said in *The Screwtape Letters*, "There are two equal and opposite errors into which our race can fall about the devils. One is to disbelieve in their existence. The other is to believe, and to feel an excessive and unhealthy interest in them. They themselves are equally pleased by both errors and hail a materialist or a magician with the same delight."[1] A big part of what makes uncertain times so uncertain is the spiritual warfare going on behind the scenes that we can't see.

What we know of this realm has been revealed to us in Scripture. For instance, we know that there is true spiritual warfare going on all around us all the time. Paul, in Ephesians 6, makes sure we know who our true enemy is and what armor God has given us for engaging in this battle. Likewise, John in this passage reveals that a true spirit of antichrist is alive and well. It is intent on defaming the person and work of Christ and on destroying the church. That is what we'll address in this chapter. We will define the term "antichrist" and how it is used in two different ways in this passage, and we'll discuss the characteristics of an antichrist spirit. I also hope to encourage you with the words of John to remain in Christ, and I hope to explain what he means by that. This will help us learn how to deal with and defeat the spirit of antichrist both in the church and in the world.

Antichrist vs. the Spirit of Antichrist (2:18-23)

What is the difference between Antichrist and antichrists? First, you have to appreciate the tenderness with which John speaks to the people. He

---

[1] C.S. Lewis. *The Screwtape Letters* (San Francisco, CA: HarperSanFrancisco Zondervan Publishing House, 2001), IX

calls them "children" in verse 18. Like a good father, he is concerned about the church and the harm and disunity false teaching can bring upon them. He is like a good shepherd watching over his flock, protecting them from wolves in sheep's clothing.

Take note of John's use of the term "last hour" in verse 18. New Testament authors, including John, used this term to refer to the end of days or the last days. Yet it has been almost 2000 years since the time of John. So how do we make sense of this?

First we must think of time, as best we can, from God's perspective. Both 2 Peter 3:8 and Psalm 90:4 say that one day is like one thousand years and one thousand years is like a day with the Lord. He doesn't reckon time the way we do. He stands sovereign over time, and He is outside of time.

Therefore, in the New Testament, the phrase "last days" or "last hour" refers to the time of the church after the resurrection of Christ. They were then, as we are now, in the last days. Why? Because Christ could come back at any time. His return is imminent. Jesus himself and the New Testament authors all give us signs or warnings about this time. They want us to stay alert, and one of the reasons to stay alert is because Satan is doing everything he can to deceive both believers and unbelievers about the person of Christ and the message of the gospel.

That's where John is coming from when he warns of an antichrist spirit. Let me now differentiate between capital "A" Antichrist and little "a" antichrists. The only difference between the terms in Greek, *antichristos* (literally anti-Messiah), is that one is singular and one is plural.

The capital "A" Antichrist was a particular individual, often in New Testament Scripture, who would be possessed by Satan and would rise up in the last days and oppose the church. He will attempt to defame Jesus, assert himself as Messiah, and, as such, deem himself worthy of worship. He will be the worst human enemy the church has ever faced. Many will die at his hand, but Christ ultimately defeats him and casts him into hell for all eternity (Revelation 19:17-21).

The little "a" antichrists John is referring to here have been around since the dawn of the church in the first century and will remain until Christ comes back. They are false teachers. They propagate a false gospel that usually either attacks the person and work of Christ or distorts the biblical requirements of salvation.

Early Church History Heresies

Dealing with this type of heresy is nothing new for the church of Jesus. There are many examples we could look at throughout the history of the church where it dealt with similar issues. My aim is not to provide a detailed analysis of each one of these issues. For our purposes, I only wish to give a very brief summary of a few of them.

In the third century, Arianism arose to challenge the nature of the person of Christ. It was an influential heresy denying the divinity of Christ, originating with the Alexandrian priest Arius (c.250– c. 336). Arianism maintained that the Son of God was created by the Father and was therefore neither coeternal with the Father, nor consubstantial, meaning of the same substance or essence of the Father. Arian was eventually condemned as a heretic at the Council of Constantinople in 381 A.D.

There was also Gnosticism which denies or minimizes the humanity of Christ. They taught that Jesus never actually "dwelt on this earth in human form."[2] It's hard to pinpoint when Gnosticism started, but there were signs of it very early on in the first century church. The gnostic thought and practice, especially of various cults of late pre-Christian and early Christian centuries, was distinguished by the conviction that matter is evil and that emancipation comes through *gnosis* (knowledge). It taught that what you did in your physical body was inconsequential. It is the spirit or soul God desires to save, not the body. This system encourages, either directly or indirectly, licentious living because ultimately the flesh will be destroyed, but God will save the soul.

Marcion was one of these Gnostics. He believed Jesus was the savior sent by God and that Paul the Apostle was his chief apostle, but he rejected the Hebrew Bible and the God of Israel. Marcionists believed that the wrathful Hebrew God was a separate and lower entity than the all-forgiving God of the New Testament. He was eventually excommunicated from the church and condemned as a heretic in 144 AD.

The early church also dealt with Judaizers. These were Jewish Christian converts who taught that Gentile Christians must be circumcised and adhere to the laws of Moses in order to be saved. Paul dealt with this issue in the New Testament both with the Apostle Peter and with the church at Galatia (Galatians 2:11-14). The Judaizers were teaching a works-based salvation contrary to the gospel taught by Jesus and the Apostles.

All false teachings in some way fall under three categories. They openly attack the deity of Christ, they deny the humanity of Christ (and thus his work on the cross), or they in some way distort the message of the gospel as it relates to salvation.

---

[2] B.K. Kuiper. *The Church in History* (Grand Rapids, MI: Wm. B. Eerdmans Publishing Co., 1988), 17

Three Characteristics of "Antichrists" or False Teachings (2:19; 22-23)

Moving back to the discussion of what John means by antichrist, John points out three characteristics of "antichrists" or false teachings in this passage. First, false teaching is demonic in nature. In John 8:44 Jesus says of Satan, "When he tells a lie, he speaks from his own nature, because he is a liar and the father of lies." The word Satan actually means "adversary." Our enemy is very good at lying. It comes from his nature. It is who he is. The first lie ever told was by Satan in the garden. His job is to defame the name of Christ, bring confusion to the gospel message, and cause doubt about the word of God.

To reiterate, all false teachings are demonic in nature. They distort the truth and oppose Christ. Do we as believers acknowledge the reality of this supernatural struggle? Do we realize there are real forces at work opposed to Christ and His church? Do we also realize that that these forces are constantly at work attempting to deceive us with the false promises of a false gospel? This makes it all the more important that we root our faith and our lives in the word of God. We should devote ourselves fully to it. We should pray for wisdom concerning it. We must learn to love it and crave it the way we crave the air we breathe. We must seek to store it in our hearts. His word along with the guidance of the Holy Spirit is the only weapon we have against these attacks.

I pose this question: If all of a sudden all the Bibles in the world disappeared, and we no longer had access to the written word of God, have you stored up enough of the gospel truth in your heart to be able to stand with confidence and joy against spiritual attacks and the lure of false gospels? I hope we have. We must hide His word, and hide it deep, in our hearts lest we be lured away by the temptations of false gospels.

Secondly, false teachers abandon or harm the church (v.19). One of the strongest defining marks of a believer is perseverance. Many Protestants, especially Baptists, believe strongly in assurance of salvation, that those who have been bought and paid for by the blood of Christ, who have repented and turned to him for salvation, will never defect from the church or leave Christ. In other words, they can never become lost again.

The Baptist Faith and Message says it like this in Article V, which is entitled, *God's Purposes of Grace*: "All true believers endure to the end. Those whom God has accepted in Christ, and sanctified by His Spirit, will never fall away from the state of grace, but shall persevere to the end. Believers may fall into sin through neglect and temptation, whereby they grieve the Spirit, impair their graces and comforts, and bring reproach on the cause of Christ and temporal judgments on themselves; yet they shall be kept by the power of God through faith unto salvation."[3]

Jesus said in John 10:25-30: "'I did tell you and you don't believe,' Jesus answered them. 'The works that I do in my Father's name testify about me. [26] But you do not believe because you are not of my sheep.[27] My sheep hear my voice, I know them, and they follow me. [28] I give them eternal life, and they will never perish. No one will snatch them out of my hand. [29] My Father, who has given them to me, is greater than all. No one is able to snatch them out of the Father's hand. [30] I and the Father are one.'"

---

[3] "V. God's Purpose of Grace", Baptist Faith and Message, Southern Baptist Convention, Accessed February, 11, 2021, https://bfm.sbc.net/bfm2000/#v-gods-purpose-of-grace.

It is clear that the eternal life of the believer is secure in the hands of Christ. We are His. This doesn't mean you won't sin or stumble. This doesn't mean you won't have periods of your life where you are disgruntled or hurt by the church. You might even for a period in your life have left the local church. It is important for us to remember that the church is full of people who are in the process of being conformed into the image of Jesus (Romans 8:29). We say hurtful things, we do things not consistent with the Christian life, and sometimes we just get church wrong. The good news is that a true believer, in the hands of Christ, will persevere: not because you are good enough or strong enough, but because Christ, your advocate and propitiation, is on your side. You are His child, and you are safe in Him. It is in His power and grace we repent, we keep fighting for truth, and we keep serving the church, the Bride of Christ.

Contrast that with what John says in verse 19, "They [meaning false teachers or unbelievers] went out from us, but they did not belong to us." These people have not just left a church and moved their membership to another. They have defected from their local, gospel-believing church, and in doing so they have spurned Christ. John says that those who do that were never in Christ to begin with.

I think this gives us two realities in today's church world of which we should be aware. First, not all who say they follow Jesus, or even emotionally act as if they love Jesus, actually do. A person's claims must be backed up with (1) right doctrine and (2) right practice. To love Christ means you believe what he taught about Himself, and you live as He commanded you to live. The painful truth about every church membership roll is that not all who say they believe in and follow Jesus actually do.

Second, not all local congregations are biblical churches. Our world and culture are full of buildings that have the word "church" on them, but they have nothing to do with what the Bible says a church is. Often false teachers will leave a congregation because either they have selfish ambitions or because a biblical church has removed them for false teaching and sin, and they will start another "church." The start of many false religions began this way. Church planting is good and biblical, but not if it is done for selfish reasons. I do not have time to go into what the marks of a true church biblically are, but just be aware that not all that glitters is gold in the church world. What a church believes and teaches about the Bible and about Jesus will tell you if it is a true church or not. When it is all said and done, an antichrist person abandons the church.

Lastly, John points out that false teachers reject Jesus and His works (v.22-23). The centerpiece of false teaching is that it always either outright denies or waters down the basics of the faith doctrinally, especially as it relates to the person and work of Jesus. They will deny that Christ was the Messiah, and they deny He was from the Father or that Jesus and the Father are one. A false teacher may have believed Jesus was important, but they stop short of believing He was God. They see Him as significant and special but not as the Savior. It is important we recognize these errors for what they are and be able to recognize them today. Like Danny Akin said in his commentary on 1 John, "It's better to be divided over the truth than to be united by error."[4]

So what are some day modern- day equivalents of the false teaching John was dealing with in the first century church? Again, I'm not trying to

---

[4] Daniel L. Akin. *Christ-Centered Exposition: Exalting Jesus in 1, 2, and 3 John*, eds. David Platt, Daniel L. Akin, and Tony Merida (Nashville, TN: B&H Publishing Group, 2014), 53

fully detail the entire belief system of these false teachings. I'm just trying to focus on what it is about Jesus they get wrong, and in what ways their message is harmful to the gospel.

I would first point out Jehovah's Witnesses. They deny the full deity and eternality of Jesus. They teach that Jesus is not Jehovah God nor is he coequal with the Father. They also teach that Jesus was a creation of God; therefore, they deny the eternal nature of Christ. They would say, "Jesus was raised from the dead, not with a physical body, but as a mighty spirit creature."[5]

There is also the rampant propagation of the Prosperity Gospel. This is a religious belief among some Christians who hold that financial blessing and physical well-being are always the will of God for them, and that faith, positive speech, and donations to religious causes will increase one's material wealth. Prosperity theology views the Bible as a contract between God and humans: if humans have faith in God, he will deliver security and prosperity. It sees Jesus as a means to an end. If you just have enough faith, Jesus will grant you all things you want: money, fame, possessions, etc.

Progressive Christianity (liberalism) is becoming more and more prevalent. Sometimes these are labeled as "red-letter Christians" who often disregard a lot of or all of the Old Testament. They do not often talk about God's wrath and justice as much as his mercy and love. They are willing to call the Bible inspired, authoritative, or sufficient but often stop short of calling it inerrant or infallible. They come to many of their conclusions about the Bible by interpreting scripture in light of culture instead of culture in light of Scripture.

---

[5] Walter Martin, *The Kingdom of the Cults*, ed. Ravi Zacharias (Bloomington, MN: Bethany House Publishers, 2003), 48

Universalism denies the need of repentance and faith in Christ as necessary for salvation. They believe all roads lead to God, and that ultimately all will be saved. There is also Moralistic Therapeutic Deism as elaborated upon by Christian Smith.[6] This views God as nothing more than a divine genie who we can call upon when we need something, but who isn't really involved in our day-to-day lives.

I could name many more, but I hope no you understand that what John was dealing with in the first century is no different than what the church still deals with today. Now that we have a basic understanding of what John meant when he talked about the spirit of antichrist involved in the false teaching of his day, and we've also discussed some modern day equivalents, let's look at three characteristics John points out of a true believer.

Three Characteristics of True Believer (2:20-21; 24-27)

First, they abide in the anointing of the Holy Spirit (v.20-21). Baptists sometimes stray away from the word *anointing* because of its charismatic connotations. The Greek word used here is *chrisma,* which is the root word from which we get the English word charisma. We also get from it the word "charismatic" which is often used to describe Pentecostal circles, but the word here is just referring to the presence of the Holy Spirit in the life of a believer. Christ promised the disciples before he left that He would send the Holy Spirit and referred to him as a comfort, a guide, a teacher, an advocate, etc.

---

[6] See Christian Smith and Melinda Lundquist Denton, *Soul Searching: The Religious and Spiritual Lives of American Teenagers* (Oxford: Oxford University Press, 2005)

I think this passage teaches us two important truths about the Spirit's presence in our life as it relates to abiding in Christ and in His Spirit, especially as it relates to false teachings. First, He guides us in all truth. In John 14:26, Jesus said of the Holy Spirit, "But the Counselor, the Holy Spirit, whom the Father will send in my name, will teach you all things and remind you of everything I have told you."

This was a promise He made to the disciples. John reiterates it here in this letter. Because of the anointing of the Holy Spirit, all of Jesus's disciples have knowledge. They have the knowledge that the Holy Spirit shared with John and that John shared with them. We also have the Holy Spirit in us as a guide and teacher to help us discern the truth. In verse 21, John affirms that even though false teaching was all around them, they indeed had access to the truth. How can he be sure of that? Because it was John, led by the Spirit, that taught it to them! Since John only shared what the Holy Spirit gave him, there was "no lie that could come from this truth". It was all true and given by the Spirit.

This is important. John had shared with them the Gospel as he had heard it from Jesus himself and received from the Holy Spirit. There was nothing else needed to supplement that truth. This is where false teachers are deceptive. They often say you need Jesus plus something, such as Jesus plus works, Jesus plus the law, or Jesus plus another special revelation. John was saying that what Jesus and the Holy Spirit had shared with him, he had freely shared with them. They had all they needed. They just needed to trust the Sprit to guide them in that truth.

Secondly, the Holy Spirit guards against error. The Holy Spirit is like a built in lie-detector for the believer. John MacArthur says that the Holy Spirit is an "illuminating guardian from deception."[7]

The false teachers of John's day claimed that John's message needed to be supplemented with special revelation or higher knowledge. This is yet another sign of false teaching. False teachers claim to have special knowledge that you need in order to be really saved, but the plot twist is that only they have that knowledge. They claim God has only shared it with them personally.

This is why abiding in the presence of the Holy Spirit is so important. We must stay in the word of God. We must trust the Holy Spirit to guide and teach us. The Holy Spirit will never reveal anything to you or anyone else that is contrary to what God has already given us in His word. It is complete as it is, and it needs nothing added to it. If someone claims something as a revelation from God, but it is either opposed to His word or adds to his word, then it is false. We must abide in the Spirit and trust His word.

The second characteristic of a true believer is that they abide steadfast in the Gospel (vv.24-26). John said that in order to combat false teaching it is all the more important for God's people to remain steadfast in his word. When John says in verse 24, "what you have heard from the beginning," he is referring to the gospel message he proclaimed to them at first.

It is important that we remember that the gospel, God's word, is a fixed truth. It is unalterable. It is unchanging. Jude 3 says, "Dear friends, although I was eager to write you about the salvation we share, I found it necessary to write, appealing to you to contend for the faith that was delivered to the saints once for all."

---

[7] John MacArthur, *The MacArthur Bible Commentary* (Nashville, TN: Thomas Nelson, 2005), 1956

Jude, like John, faced false teaching. Because people in the church were accepting false teaching, Jude wrote his letter to warn them. He says three very important things about the Gospel here. First, it was delivered to the early church by the Apostles. They didn't come up with this truth; it was given to them by God through the Apostles. Second, they must contend for it. They must fight to preserve it. Third, it is "once for all," (Jude 3). It was given once. Nothing needs to be added to it or deleted from it. This goes back to the doctrine of the sufficiency of Scripture: Scripture is complete, it is finished, and it is fixed for all time. It is all you needed to be saved, and it is all you'll ever need to persevere in salvation. Stand in it. Remain in it. John makes this clear in verse 25. The reward of remaining in it, of holding fast to it, is eternal life.

The third and final characteristic of a true believer is that they abide in the truth. To put it another way, we remain in Jesus (v. 27). With the Holy Spirit and the Word of God as your guard and guide, walk in the truth. Live it.

Abiding in Jesus is a lifestyle. It is something, by the power of the Holy Spirit, that you do every single day. This life throws so much at us, such as financial distress, the pain of losing those you love, sickness and pain, and broken relationships. We need a hope that is greater than us and greater than this life. Our hope is glory. It is that one day we will see the face of Jesus. That is what it means to abide in the truth. You walk in it. You live in it. If need be, you give your life for it. That is why false teaching is so harmful and so damaging. It has eternal ramifications. It takes the things of this life, dresses them up, and offers them to us as if they can fix all our problems. False teaching says, "Jesus is great, but you know what else you need?" Then it feeds you another lie.

No matter what happens in this life, here is our hope. THE GOSPEL IS ENOUGH. JESUS IS ENOUGH. False teaching says you need one more thing. The gospel says that Jesus is all you need. As you hold on to Jesus, He holds on to you. Even if your grip falters, His never will. He is enough. Dear Christian, we must continue to abide in Him in a world full of antichrists.

Chapter 5| Proclaim Hope for the Hopeless
1 John 2:28- 3:3

Hope is a precious word. Defined, it means to "cherish or desire with anticipation; to want something to happen or be true."[1] As a kid, I had many hopes. I had hoped to grow taller one day. That didn't happen. I'm only five feet six inches. I'd hope to hit a home run in Little League. That also didn't happen, although I came close a couple of times. I had hoped to start on the varsity football team in high school. That did happen, but I'm still not sure how. These are the kinds of hopes a kid has.

I was a huge Atlanta Braves fan as a kid as well. My favorite player was pitcher and future hall of famer John Smoltz. At times, he seemed unhittable on the mound, especially in 1996 when he won the Cy Young award. If you watched baseball in the 1990s, you know that the Braves went on a streak where they won several divisional pennants in a row. They

---

[1] "Hope", Merriam-Webster, Accessed February 11, 2021, https://www.merriam-webster.com/dictionary/hope.

were perennial playoff contenders with one of the deadliest pitching rotations in Major League Baseball which included future hall of famers Tom Glavine and Greg Maddux. My biggest hope as a fan of the Braves was to see them win the World Series. They made it to the World Series five times between 1991-1999. They lost the first two to the Minnesota Twins and Toronto Blue Jays. But the third time in 1995 they won by beating the Cleveland Indians in six games. My hopes had finally became reality, and I was ecstatic! I remember the thrill of watching my team win it all. They were the best in the world. But that excitement fades away pretty quickly. I had realized my hope as a fan, but I wasn't satisfied. I hoped they could win more. I hoped they could win every year. Of course they didn't win it every year. No team does. Hope is a fragile thing if the only things we hope for are in this world.

I believe for those who follow Jesus that a more accurate definition of hope is to "expect with confidence." R.C. Sproul defines hope by saying, "Hope is called the anchor of the soul (Hebrews 6:19), because it gives stability to the Christian life. But hope is not simply a 'wish'; rather, it is that which latches on to the certainty of the promises of the future God has made."[2]

We have all battled hopelessness. At the very least, we have all had moments where our hope was clouded. The craziness of raising kids, keeping up at our jobs, and all the demands of our time and attention often take our focus off of our ultimate hope. Some of you may struggle with doubt, depression, or understand the process of trying to overcome a devastating loss. My goal in this chapter is to simply remind you of the hope

---

[2] R.C. Sproul. *The Purpose of God: An Exposition of Ephesians* (Scotland, UK: Christian Focus Publications, 1994), 40

we have in Christ. If you are reading this and feel hopeless for some reason, I hope today that God would help peel back the shadows just a little bit and give you a glimpse of His glory so that your hope may begin to be restored.

Hebrews 11: 1 says that our faith is the "reality of what is hoped for." Our faith is anchored in something that is not merely a wish or a desire. It is anchored in a reality. It is anchored in a deep, unchanging truth. It is rooted in something that we anticipate with utmost confidence. It is held fast by something of which God has assured us of in His word. According to 1 John 2:28-3:3, our hope is anchored in the return of Christ, and that truth should make all the difference in how we love and live.

Hope to Stand Bold and Unashamed (2:28)

This whole section of 1 John focuses on our hope in light of the return of Christ. In verse 28, we see John repeat his desire that believers abide in Christ. Often in scripture, important concepts are repeated over and over again. This is true in 1 John. Repeatedly we see him exhorting the church to abide, abide, abide. And just when you think he has made his point, he reminds them once more to abide in Christ. To John, abiding in Christ accomplished two things. First, it protected believers from false teaching. As long as they were abiding in Him and His word, they would be less likely to fall victim to false teaching. Second, abiding in Christ increased their hope. It increased their longing for Jesus. To abide in Christ and in His presence gives us assurance. According to verse 28, it also gives us boldness and confidence so that we might not be ashamed at His return. Abiding is something we actively pursue. It is not passive.

Salvation is so secure because Christ is constantly holding onto us and because, through abiding, we are constantly holding onto Him. For true believers, both of these realities will always be true. For false believers, like the ones John has been describing, they will eventually fade from abiding in Christ because they never belonged to Christ to begin with. Without Jesus holding onto us, we can never in our own strength hold onto him.

Abiding in Christ gives us hope in two things specifically. First, we can have hope that He will indeed return. That is what John is implying in this text. Jesus will return one day. Everyone on earth will experience this monumental, universe-altering event. Everyone will bow to him. All will acknowledge Him as King. For each individual, Christ's return will either mean eternal judgement and separation from God or eternal redemption. Each person will either cover his or her face in shame, or they will lift their eyes to gaze on their redeemer. Christ will return.

Secondly, abiding in Christ gives us hope that at His return we will not have anything of which we are ashamed. For those without Christ, their shame is not covered. They will be like Adam and Eve hiding in the garden of Eden frantically sewing fig leaves together to cover themselves for fear of being exposed to God's glory and holiness. At his return, you will either run to him in joy or from him in fear. You will either try to flee your righteous Judge or run to your good Father. But for believers, our hope rests in the fact that Christ has covered our shame. He nailed our sin to the cross and took God's wrath upon Himself for us. He did this so that we might stand unashamed before Him. We have hope that at Christ's return the Father will accept us, not because of any good deed we have done, but because of the work of Christ on our behalf.

If you feel like your hope has run out, take confidence in this: If you belong to Christ, God the Father will not turn you away. In His arms are rest and peace and comfort this world has never known. In Him, there is the removal of all pain and sorrow and depression. Brother and sister, rest in that hope. I'll say more about this further down.

Hope That Frees Us to Pursue Righteousness (2:29)

During the summer harvest, many farmers get to see and taste the fruit of their labor. When a seed is put in the ground, the final product, hopefully, is something that is satisfying, filling, and enjoyable. The hard work of farming--planting, watering, weeding, watering some more, weeding some more, pruning, and watering again-- pays off when you see fruit on the vine and get to enjoy it at your own table. The harvest is proof that the plant or vine was rooted in what the plant needed most to grow.

It is the same with our hope. If our hope is rooted in Christ, then the fruit of hope is righteousness. Our hope will make righteousness a habit. That is why John says in 1 John 2:29, "Everyone who does what is right has been born of Him." The word "born" here is the same Greek word Jesus used with Nicodemus in John 3 when He explained to him that a person must be "born" again to enter the kingdom of Heaven. Those who are born again bear the fruit of righteousness because Christ, the anchor of our hope, is righteous. We can have hope that if we are abiding in Christ, and if we are rooted in Him, we will bear the fruit of righteousness.

The truth is that before you were born again, Christian, you were a slave of sin. It wasn't just that you didn't want to pursue righteousness, but you were unable to pursue it. Christ frees you to not only be able to pursue righteousness but to desire it as well. To belong to Christ means to desire righteousness. He changes our heart so that we now desire righteousness, and we bear righteous fruit.

If my hope rests in my own ability to pursue God and live for Him, then that hope will fail. I have no hope in and of myself to be able to do that. However, if my hope rests in Christ and His righteousness, that hope will not only carry me through this life, but it will carry me throughout all eternity. That kind of hope will never fail. It is an exhausting exercise to try to please God by your own efforts. To root your life in any hope except for Jesus means you will bear the fruit of hopelessness. We should build our hope on Christ and Christ alone.

Hope in God's Love That Saved Us (1 John 3:1)

As I read 1 John 3:1, I can almost picture John's astonishment as he recalls the great truth of God's love for him. The almighty Creator of the universe loves us. We are children of our heavenly Father. John is utterly amazed by this truth. To be a child of God is the wildest thing in the world to Him. What a great cure for hopelessness this great truth is!

Think about this. We all have an earthly father. Not all of us had good experiences with our earthly fathers. But if you are a believer, John says you also have a heavenly Father. We bear his name. The book of Revelation implies that he has a name for you that only He knows (Revelation 2:17). He is crazy about you! To John, the kind of love God has for His children is astounding. It is an out-of-this-world kind of love, and it is that love that enables us to be called His child. It is His love that came first. It is His love that found us. It is His love that whispered our name when we were his enemies, and it called us out of our sin and rescued us from death. It is His love that even now is sustaining us, protecting us, guiding us, teaching us, refining us, purifying us, disciplining us, and perfecting us. Furthermore, one day, it is His love that will rescue us for all eternity and bring us home to be with Him. That is something in which to place your hope! One of the reasons we long for the return of Christ is that we will finally be reunited with our heavenly Father. What a great hope!

We have a hope in something greater than ourselves. According to John, we are aliens in this world. We are not at home. In the same way the world rejected Jesus, it will reject his followers, too. There will always be friction between followers of Christ and the world. That is why, for those who are believers, misplaced hope is so devastating. Misplaced hope directs our affections away from our heavenly home.

John tells us to place our hope in the fact that we are God's child. If we are His child, we are loved by Him. Therefore, if we are loved by Him, He will one day bring us home. There we will finally see Him as He is, so rest in this hope. You have been adopted by a King, and you have a royal inheritance waiting on you.

Hope That We Will One Day Be with and Like Christ (3:2)

Romans 8:28-30 makes it very clear that the primary purpose of every believer is to be conformed to the image of Christ. The Bible says that believers will reign with Jesus and be like Him one day, but the hard truth is that, for now, we will also suffer like Him. In 1 John 3:2, John is explaining that same purpose. He is offering hope to the churches by affirming what we will be one day. We are even now God's children, but what we will be at

His return hasn't been revealed yet. In providing us salvation, God isn't just simply rescuing His people; He is transforming them daily. As Paul says in 2 Corinthians 5:17, "Therefore, if anyone is in Christ, he is a new creation." We are daily being made new. Every day, by His grace, God is changing us from the inside out. One of the promises of Scripture is that not only does God give us new hearts when He saves us; He also will one day give us new bodies. This is the wonderful doctrine of glorification. God's plan of redemption for those who trust Christ includes the redemption of your physical body one day.

Right now, in this life, it is easy to lose hope. We look at ourselves falling apart, and it is hard to imagine a life devoid of the painful things we experience here and now. What will it be like to be free of pain and sickness? What will it be like to experience life in bodies that never grow old and die? How exhilarating will it be to have the freedom to love without the risk of a broken heart? There will be no grip of sin, no fear of death, and no sadness or mourning. There will be no doubt about the future and no worries about tomorrow.

We can't conceive of a world without those things. Our reality right now includes death, sin, mourning, pain, and sickness. As soon as you are born, you begin to die. Your heart will only beat so many times. Your lungs will only take in so many precious breaths. As we age, our hearing dulls and our eyesight fades. What is to hope for in the midst of all of these stark realities?

Danny Akin says that there is a tension in the Christian life. We live in the midst of an already, but not yet, moment. He says, "We do not yet realize or experience all the benefits that salvation promises for God's children. We are still in process, a work under construction, a divine work of art that is not yet complete."[3] Again, how do we maintain hope in the midst of an already, but not yet, moment?

John says that we hope in a resurrection. First, we believe in the resurrection of Jesus. When John says, "We will be like Him" (1 John 3:2), he is pointing back to the resurrection of Jesus. His resurrection is the guarantee of our own resurrection. 1 Corinthians 15:20-21 says, "Christ has been raised from the dead, the first fruits of those who have fallen asleep. For since death came through a man, the resurrection of the dead also comes through a man." Our belief in the resurrection of Jesus is vital to our hope. Because He was raised, we will be raised too. When He resurrected, He obtained a glorified and incorruptible nature not subject to the decay of earthly flesh. Paul says of the resurrection body in 1 Corinthians 15:43-44 that it is incorruptible, glorious, powerful, and spiritual-- yet physical. That is what Christ is now, and that is what we will be one day.

That is why we look forward to His return. Because then we will "...be like Him because we will see Him as He is," (1 John 3:2). In Psalm 17:15, the psalmist must have been reflecting on this truth when he wrote, "But I will see your face in righteousness; when I awake, I will be satisfied with Your presence." We will not fully be like Christ because we are not divine. We are not omnipresent, all-knowing, or all-powerful, but we will be like Him in that we will "be morally without sin, intellectually without falsehood and error, physically without weakness or imperfection, and filled continually with the Holy Spirit never to grieve Him again."[4]

---

[3] Daniel L. Akin. *Christ-Centered Exposition: Exalting Jesus in 1, 2, and 3 John*, eds. David Platt, Daniel L. Akin, and Tony Merida (Nashville, TN: B&H Publishing Group, 2014), 60

[4] Robert W. Yarbrough, study notes on 1 John 3:2, in *ESV Study Bible* (Wheaton, IL: Crossway, 2008),2433

This is crazy good news for us. Our hope is fueled by the fact that we will see Him as He is, and in seeing Him, we will be like Him. Oh, how we should long for that day! What will it be like to be completely remade? We will cast off the filth of this life like a garment and be clothed in the glory of Christ. Do you long to see Him? I know I do. I sometimes find myself from time to time looking up at the sky and picturing what it will be like when He comes again. That is something in which we can hope. His return is as certain as the rising and the setting of the sun. One day we will go to sleep with the worries of the world on our minds, and we will wake up and see Him. Do you hope for that day?

Hope That Causes Us to Walk in Purity (3:3)

The final point about hope I want to make is that a hope rooted in the person of Christ, His death, burial, resurrection, and return, changes the way we live. To live in anticipation of the return of Christ makes a difference in our walk. My family and I take a trip to the beach every year in September. My in-laws rent a beach house, and we all go down to Gulf Shores, Alabama, and pile in. It's on the calendar every year for a year in advance. As soon as we get back from the trip, the next one gets booked. We are very serious about this trip. The closer in the year it gets to this trip, the more our anticipation of it grows. When winter changes into spring, and spring into summer, we get excited because we know the trip to the beach is drawing near. In August, I can have a bad day, but it doesn't matter because I know my trip to the beach is coming up. If I get tired and worn down, which with three kids is inevitable, I can say to myself "But the beach is only a few weeks away, and I can make it until then." I'm sure many of you do the same thing. If the anticipation of a trip to the beach can motivate us that much, how much more ought the return of the Lord!

As the people of the Lord anxiously awaiting His return, we are called to walk in purity. 1 John 3:3 says it this way, "Everyone who has this hope in Him purifies himself just as He is pure." To be pure means to be free of contamination. What is it that contaminates us before the Lord? It is our sin, and who has removed that sin from those who hope in Christ? Jesus has, by His death on the cross and resurrection from the tomb. One day we will be like him, but for now we pursue purity.

But how do we do this? How can sinful people live pure lives? Does this mean we must work in order to keep our salvation? No, it certainly does not. R.C. Sproul says there are two heresies regarding pursuing purity. One he calls quietism. This is the belief that says, "Let go and let God." It says that nothing is required of me, no effort on my part, in order to be perfected. God will do it all. My only job is to stay out of His way, do nothing, and God will take care of everything in spite of my inactivity.

The other heresy Sproul calls activism. Activism is the belief that says, "Yes God has saved me, but it is completely up to me now to live as I ought." It is a "pull yourself up by your own bootstraps" mentality. It views justification as God's work but sanctification as mine.[5]

Both of these views are wrong. Neither give us a biblical picture of what it means to walk in purity. Paul in Philippians 2: 12-15 gives us a glimpse of how this works:

---

[5] R.C. Sproul and Nathan W. Bingham, "Should I 'Let Go and Let God'?", Ligonier, Published on June 27, 2018, https://www.ligonier.org/blog/should-i-let-go-and-let-god/.

"So then my dear friends, just as you have always obeyed, not only in my presence, but now even more in my absence, *work out your own salvation with fear and trembling.* For it is God who is working in you, enabling you both *to desire* and *to work out* His good purpose. Do everything without grumbling and arguing, so that you may be blameless and pure, Children of God who are faultless in a crooked and perverted generation, among whom you shine like stars in the world," (emphasis mine).

Our hope in the return of the Lord motivates us to live as both John and Paul have commanded us to live. God enables us to do as He has called us to do. If He has called us to live in purity, then he gives us the strength to do it. We are called to do good works, which the Lord has prepared ahead of time for us to do (Ephesians 2:9).

So do we work out our own salvation and strive to live in purity? Yes, we do. Does God work in us enabling us to live out a life of purity? Yes, he does. The answer to both questions is the same because both are true. The kind of hope that we as believers have is an active hope. We actively pursue righteousness. It's not the kind of hope that sits back and wishes for things to happen, but it is the kind of hope that knows for certain Christ is coming back. And if He is coming back, we ought to be found doing what He has called you and I to do. In doing that, we must have hope that He will give us the courage and strength required to do it.

To that end, we wait. We wait with hope that one day we will stand before Him blameless and unashamed. We, even now, pursue righteousness and live in the fact that you and I are a loved child of God. We pursue purity and live as stars and beacons of light for the gospel in a dark and dying world. We wait for the day of his returning, knowing then we will be as we were made to be. We will see him and see ourselves as we should be for the first time. We will walk on the new, holy ground of the new heavens and new earth. We will run without becoming weary. We will live without fear of death. We will love without the fear of heartache and loss. We will inherit the Kingdom, and Christ himself will walk with us forever. Let that kind of hope be a cure for our hopelessness.

Chapter 6| Remember Why Christ Came

1 John 3:4-10

I.   Christ Came to Defeat Sin on the Cross (v.5-6)

II.   Christ Came to Destroy the Works of Satan (v.7-8)

III.   Christ Came to Impart a Distinguishing Love (v.9-10)

A Working Definition of Sin

The previous chapter of this book focused largely on the second appearing of Christ. We live in anticipation of his return. We will finally see Him, and we will be like Him. His resurrection guarantees our own, and we will be with Him forever. This chapter, instead of pointing forward to the return of Christ to encourage believers, will look back at the first advent of Christ. It seems like John not only wants the church to focus on the return of Christ, but he also wants them to remember why Jesus came in the first place. Why is this? I believe John wants the people to understand that sin, which had so bound them before, no longer has any power over them.

He instructed them in 1 John 3:3 to be pure. Because Christ is indeed coming back, we are motivated to live as we ought. And the reason we can live that way, John says, is because Christ has demolished sin's stronghold over God's people. We defined sin in chapter 2, but now let's look at another dimension of it.

As believers, our lives ought not be marked or defined by sin. If Christ has indeed paid for our sins, and if He is coming back, we ought to live a life not characterized by sin. The Greek phrase translated in verse four as "commits sin" gives the idea of someone who has made habitual sinning a lifestyle. It is a person defined by a life of sin. We are all indeed broken. We all still sin. But a true believer's life ought not to be defined by sin. We confess our sin, we mourn our sin, and we seek daily to crush our sin. Sin is our great enemy, and it is our primary problem.

John in verse four of chapter three defines sin as "breaking of law." What law? It is the law of God. Sin is anything not compatible with God's laws or God's standards. In its truest sense, sin is rebellion. It is rebellion against God and his ways, will, and law. To sin is to live your life in a way that either says, "There is no God and, therefore, no law," or it is to say, "I'm aware that there is (or might be) a God who has a standard, but I set my own standard and will live the way I choose." The essence of sin is the hatred of God and His law written both in His word and in our own moral conscience. Our problem as humans is that we are natural-born transgressors of the law. We are rebels, and we are enemies of God in our fallen state. The Bible says in Ephesians 2 that we are dead in our sins. We are slaves to sin. We can't follow God's law, nor do we desire to follow it.

One other way to view sin is that it is cosmic, personal treason against the God of the universe. As Creator, God is sovereign over all things. He sets the rules. He makes the laws. To sin is an act of treason against your King and Creator.

Sin is the bad news part of the gospel. We all have done it. We all fall short of God's standard. We all were at one time slaves to sin. The problem of sin is the primary reason Christ came, so let's begin to discuss this along with two other reasons that John points out Christ came.

Christ Came to Defeat Sin on the Cross (3:5-6)

One of the primary reasons for the first coming of Jesus was to defeat sin on the cross. We needed forgiveness, and Christ died so that we might receive that forgiveness. Christ came to take away the sins of His people. This was the message heralded from the very beginning of John the Baptist's ministry. His message went very quickly from "Repent! For the Kingdom of heaven has come near," (Matthew 3:2) to "Here is the Lamb of God, who takes away the sins of the world," (John 1:29). The death of Jesus paid our ransom. For those in Christ, their sins are not counted against them because Jesus has already been punished for them.

When we say that Jesus has paid for our sins, we are not speaking in generalities. We are proclaiming with the Apostle Paul in the book of Colossians that our certificate of debt has been nailed to the cross with Christ (Colossians 2:14). In Christ, God poured out his holy wrath for our sin upon Jesus instead of us. On the cross, a real transaction took place. The prophet Isaiah, speaking of Jesus, said, "He was pierced for our transgressions, crushed because of our iniquities; punishment for our peace was on Him, and we are healed by His wounds. We all went astray like sheep; we all have turned to our own way; and the Lord has punished Him for the iniquity of us all." If there was one biblical truth I could pound into the hearts of God's people, it is this: Your sin debt was very real, and Christ paid it.

Only Jesus could do this. Why is that? Because there was no sin found in Him. He was sinless. He is righteous and pure. Only He was qualified to pay the debt we owe. He was the only acceptable offering that could be offered up to God in our place. He alone could be our substitute on the cross. Paul says in 2 Corinthians 5:21, "He made the one who did not know sin to be sin for us, so that we might become the righteousness of God in Him." The main reason that sin is not compatible with the Christian life is because it is not compatible with the work of Jesus on the cross. Jesus didn't just die on the cross so we might be forgiven of sin, but He died so that our bondage to sin would be broken forever. Follow John's logic here in 1 John 3:5-6. Because Christ destroyed the work of sin in us, and because Christ Himself is sinless, His people should not live lives characterized by habitual sin. The influence that sin had over us has been broken. We are no longer slaves to sin but slaves to righteousness. What does this mean? It means that we as believers in Christ ought not live lives characterized by habitual sin.

Jesus died to sanctify us. Before trusting in Christ, our struggle was against God and His law. Now our struggle is against sin. There is an old Puritan word for this working out of sin in our lives. They called it the mortification of our sins. This means that we deny ourselves of our old sinful appetites and passions. We constantly and daily crush sin by the power of Christ. Christ's death on the cross gives us power to overcome what once mastered us-- our sin.

John makes something else crystal clear here. He says in verse 6, "Everyone who sins [habitually] has not seen Him or known Him." To John, to continue to live a life characterized by sin is a sign that that person was never in Christ to begin with. It sounds harsh. We all struggle from time to time with sin. We all fall. But I don't believe that is what John is talking about here. He was talking about people during his time who claimed to follow Jesus but were either living in sin or promoting false teaching. Their lives were defined by habitual sin, and they were unrepentant in it. To put it plainly, John says that those who live in unrepentant sin are not followers of Jesus. Christ came, primarily, to defeat sin, but he also came to destroy the works of Satan.

Christ Came to Destroy the Works of Satan (3:7-8)

John admonished the church in verse 7 to "Let no one deceive you." John knew how easy it is for people to be led astray by false teaching. False teaching isn't always bold and blatant; it more often than not is subtle lies that slowly erode the fundamentals of the faith.

This is exactly how the Communist Party in Romania post-World War Two rose to power. Subtle lies and subtle revisions to history were all it took to shape Romania into a Communist country. Trevin Wax, in his book *This is Our Time: Everyday Myths in Light of the Gospel*, says that "Communist leaders fashioned a myth."[1] He goes on to explain that:

"The revolutionaries knew the way to consolidate and maintain their power was to control the way the Romanian story was told. It wasn't enough to flex their political muscle; if they [the Communist Party] were to succeed long-term, they would need to capture the Romanian imagination. And so they decided to retell Romania's

---

[1] Trevin Wax, *This is Our Time: Everyday Myths in Light of the Gospel* (Nashville: B&H Books, 2017), 7

story and rewire the Romanian people, to make clear that the Communists were the heroes, not the bad guys. Romania's history was to be reinvented as if it were a long struggle toward the Communist vision of freedom. All the books needed to be rewritten."[2]

Just as Communism was a myth that needed to be pierced by the gospel, so it is with all false teaching. False teaching is dangerous because false theology leads to bad practices in the church. Doctrinal impurity leads to moral impurity.

John, in this passage, is calling believers to a higher standard. He is calling for them to do what is right, thus proving to whom it was they belonged: Christ Jesus. Instead of sin being our habit, righteousness should be. It should flow from you like water from a fountain. If the Righteous One, Christ, has transformed and changed your heart, then righteous words and actions should flow from that. And it is Jesus who sets the standard for righteousness.

Again, Christ destroyed our bondage to sin. We are no longer bound by it. But there is an enemy that still remains, and his name is Satan. John says in verse 8 that the "one who commits (practices) sin is of the Devil." John equates habitual sinning to being aligned with Satan. Satan is the source of all deception and false teaching. The Devil has been sinning for a long time. He is the original rebel. It was his deception that led Adam and Eve, and thus all of humanity, to death. To make a practice of sin is to live a life resembling the original sinner, Satan.

---

[2] Wax, *This is Our Time*, 7

We should also keep this in mind: Satan has absolutely nothing to lose. He is doomed, and there is no hope for him. His only job is your destruction. He has nothing else to do with the time he has left but to defame the name of Christ and to destroy His Bride, the Church. And he is relentless and restless in doing this.

That is why we must remember that Christ has already defeated Satan. It was one of the primary reasons He came. This was a fulfilling of a promise that God made to Adam and Eve all the way back in Genesis 3:14-15, which says, "Then the Lord God said to the serpent: Because you have done this, you are cursed more than any livestock and more than any wild animal. You will move on your belly and eat dust all the days of your life. I will put hostility between you and the woman, and between your seed and her seed. He will strike your head, and you will strike his heel."

Satan has been a crushed foe since the beginning of time. Christ's death on the cross fulfilled this promise. Yes, Satan struck his heel, but Christ crushed his head. Sin no longer has power over a believer, and neither are we subject to the tyranny of Satan. Satan's ultimate defeat will culminate in his eternal banishment to hell. Then all of his works of deceiving the church, persecuting the saints, stirring up rebellion, temptation, and instigating all false teachers will all be banished with him (Revelation 20:7-10).

What is the ultimate proof that Jesus has defeated sin and the work of Satan on the cross? It is the testimony of the empty tomb. Christ has risen to eternal life, and Satan, already defeated by Christ on the cross, will be banished into eternal death.

Let's turn our attention now to what Christ came to impart.

Christ Came to Impart a Distinguishing Love (3:9-10)

John is clear in 1 John 3:9 that those who are God's children do not continue in habitual sin. That is, they do not continue in a life of sin. John proves this first by explaining that to go on sinning is contrary to the work of Christ on the cross: He came and died to defeat the power of sin and Satan over us. The truth is that we are no longer bound internally by sin or externally by Satan. We are free to pursue righteousness! The work of Christ on the cross frees us, and the work of the Spirit in us enables us to live rightly. That's what being "born of God" means in verse 9. We cannot continue in sin because we have experienced a new birth. We are new creatures with a new nature. In 2 Corinthians 5:17 Paul says, "Therefore, if anyone is in Christ, he is a new creation; old things have passed away, and look, new things have come."

John then says in verse 9 that "His seed remains in him." Think about this: John is saying that a believer cannot continue in his sin because God himself has taken up residence in him. God has sent His Spirit to abide in his children. The new you loathes sin and loves righteousness. I want to be clear here. This does not mean that believers never sin. That would misrepresent this passage and go against what John taught earlier in the letter that Christ is faithful and just to forgive our sins. What John means here is that our lives are no longer marked by pleasure in sin but by a struggling towards righteousness. You are either a child of Satan or a child of God, and you can't be both.

This should comfort those of us who claim to be children of God. Our righteousness is not our own, but it is a gift of God in the new birth. Our destiny as God's children is set. He will make us more and more like Christ

(Romans 8:28-29). John goes on to say that the most evident way you can tell someone has experienced the new birth is the love shown to their brothers and sisters in Christ.

Our love for each other is a distinguishing mark and a distinguishing love different from what you see in the world. We ought to take our love for each other seriously. It was something foremost in the mind of Jesus the day before dying on the cross. Just look at what Jesus says in John 15:9-17:

> "As the Father has loved Me, I have also loved you. Remain in my love. If you keep my commands you will remain in my love, just as I have kept My Father's commands and remain in His love. I have spoken these things to you so that My joy may be in you and your joy may be complete. This is My command: Love one another as I have loved you. No one has greater love that this, that someone would lay down his life for his friends. You are My friends if you do what I command you. I do not call you slaves anymore, because a slave doesn't know what his master is doing. I have called you friends, because I have made known to you everything I have heard from My Father. You did not choose Me, but I chose you. I appointed you that you should go out and produce fruit and that your fruit should remain, so that whatever you ask the Father in my name, He will give you. This is what I command you: Love one another."

It's amazing that John makes it this simple for us. There are only two questions for the church to consider to separate those who follow Christ from those who do not: 1. Do you strive to do what is right? 2. Do you love your brothers and sisters in Christ? Holy Spirit-empowered righteousness and a self-sacrificing love for one another are the hallmarks of true Christianity. We act like our Father in heaven when we do this. He does what is right, for He can do no other. And He loves passionately and sacrificially. Ought not we as His children do the same? Shouldn't we want to be more like our Father?

We look across the aisle every Sunday and see people different from us. They are from different walks of life, at different stages of life, and come from different socio-economic statuses. We do not always agree or see eye-to-eye about everything. We don't talk the same, vote the same, or have the same passions or gifts. It's the love we have been called to that is the unifying factor. It is a radical, self-sacrificing love that distinguishes believers from the world.

What does this love look like? It sacrifices for the good of others. It warns brothers and sisters of sin and helps pull them out of it when they fall. It mourns with those who mourn and rejoices with those who rejoice. It takes food to the hungry and clothes to the naked. It speaks the truth in love and clearly identifies sin for the sake of each other's eternal soul. It comforts the sick and dying. It prays for and visits the persecuted and suffering. It links arms with other brothers and sisters for the sake of the Great Commission.

To put it plainly, it is a love that this world has never seen. And that is why Christ came. He came to destroy sin, to defeat Satan, and to give us a distinguishing love. All of this is made possible by the cross.

Chapter 7| Live Love: Truth in Action
1 John 3:10-18

The year is 2020. As I write this, our country is responding to a new strain of the coronavirus called COVID-19. The World Health Organization has just recently labeled it a global pandemic. Many schools have shut down. Restaurants, clubs, and many other places of public gathering have been asked to close or greatly reduce hours. The government has asked that gatherings of more than ten people be cancelled. All of this has been done in order to "flatten the curve."[1] In order to stop a pandemic, people must distance themselves socially. They must limit their contact with the surrounding world.

Of course, people respond to crisis in different ways. Crises, as a matter of fact, have a way of displaying both the loving nature of people and also exposing the ugly selfishness contained in every human heart. For many during this time of pandemic, love is on display. They are checking on their neighbors. They are limiting contact with those around them. They are self-quarantining in order to prevent the spread of the disease. Others, however, are being selfish. They are descending on stores and wiping out

---

[1] "What is 'Flattening the Curve'?", WebMD, revised on February 3, 2021, https://www.webmd.com/lung/qa/what-is-flattening-the-curve

their stocks of toilet paper, canned goods, water, and hand sanitizer. They are hoarding up supplies in case the pandemic lasts a long time to make sure they have all they need. Meanwhile, many others will have to go without, especially those not able to get out during this time to get supplies for themselves. Both love and the absence of it are on display when times get rough.

So far in 1 John, we have seen that love is a central theme. *Agapao*, or one of its variations, is used well over forty times in the letter of 1 John alone. We are going to talk abundantly about love as we delve further into John's letter, but for this chapter, I want to focus on three specific things John says about love in these nine verses from chapter 3. He makes it clear that love has been declared and evident from the beginning, he reminds us that the absence of love is hatred, and he emphasizes that one of the core aspects of love in action is sacrifice.

Love's Message Has Been Declared from the Beginning (3:10-11)

There are two important truths about love to learn from verses 10 and 11. First, we see from verse 10 that love for each other is a sign to the world that we are of God. We show that we are children of God by faithfully loving each other. This is the heart of a genuine Christian. The gospel of the Lord Jesus has united us as one family. All those who have trusted Christ have been adopted into God's family. We are co-heirs with Christ. Our love for each other should run deep. I've discussed this at length in previous chapters, but it is worth repeating: Believers ought to love each other.

The second truth about love that John acknowledges is that his message to the church has always included a command to love each other. Since the very beginning of creation, God has been pouring forth His love. Creation is the canvas displaying the love of God. It's a beautiful picture in Genesis 2. God, the mighty Creator of all things in the universe, gets down in the dirt and forms man with his very hands. After forming him, he raises his face up to his own and breathes life into him. His very life transferred to the man. This is love: an imparting of life to another. John says in 1 John 3:11 that this is the message he has proclaimed to the church since the beginning. Through the gospel, John has declared the love of God to them. The love of God displayed in the death, burial, and resurrection of Jesus is the message they had heard from John. It's the message God used to draw them to repentance.

This message about love for each other is not something unique to John's message. It is all throughout the New Testament:

- Show family affection to one another with brotherly love. Outdo one another in showing honor, (Romans 12:10).
- Do not owe anyone anything, except to love one another, for the one who loves another has fulfilled the law, (Romans 13:8).
- For you were called to be free, brothers; only don't use this freedom as an opportunity for the flesh, but serve one another through love, (Galatians 5:13).
- And may the Lord cause you to increase and overflow with love for one another and for everyone, (1 Thessalonians 3:12).
- And let us be concerned about one another in order to promote love and good works, (Hebrews 10:24).

- ...love one another earnestly from a pure heart, (1 Peter 1:22b).

The message of love for each other can't be emphasized enough. It is one of the central themes of all the New Testament writers. It is one of the primary ways we as believers display the wonder of the new birth to the world. The gospel of the Lord Jesus takes a people who at one point were natural enemies and it unites them in love. It is a love that transcends all barriers the world would put between us. It overcomes all racial, cultural, socio-economic, linguistic, and ethnic barriers.

In the summer of 2019, six others and I traveled to South Asia to share the gospel. Our mission was simple. We collaborated with a local American missionary and seven local Christians and church planters who could speak the native language and English. They served as our translators. Our goal was to spend seven days trekking very steep and mountainous terrain in order to go to hard-to-reach villages to share the gospel home to home. I expected this trip to be difficult both spiritually and physically, but nothing could have prepared me for exactly how hard it would end up being. On the first day, I knew that I had grossly underestimated the physical toll this trek was going to take on my body. It was the beginning of the rainy season. Leeches were everywhere, and they often would find their way under your clothes and into your socks. The bites didn't hurt, but they injected an anti-coagulant into your blood which made the bites bleed for hours. We ran out of bandages very soon and ended up using duct tape to cover the bites to get them to stop bleeding-- a new use for duct tape for me.

We would often spend hours each day trekking straight up a very steep hillside, straight down it the next day (which was just as difficult!), and back up again the next day just to reach the next village. It was treacherous, it was exhausting, and it was physically and emotionally deflating. But each day we made it to our destination. Each day we shared the gospel. Each day people who had never heard the gospel received it with joy and trusted Christ alone as Savior. All in all, almost 300 people came to know the Lord on this trek, and several churches were started.

I look back on that trip now, and two things stick out to me. First, I have never been more tired and exhausted in my life, but I still recall this trip with joy. I look fondly back on those seven dangerous and exhausting days. As a matter of fact, I long to go back. I would do it all over again. Secondly, I recall with great fondness the friendships we developed over those seven days with our translators. We had absolutely nothing but Jesus in common with these people, but I would consider them all brothers who I love dearly. I still keep in touch with some of them. What is it that could possibly take one of the most dangerous and energy-sapping moments of my life and turn it into one of the most joyful experiences I have ever had? It is just one word: love. The gospel transcended every barrier between those local Christian translators and me. By the end of the trip they weren't just translators; they were friends and brothers and co-laborers in the gospel. That's the power of Christian love, and that is why love for each other is so central to the message of John and the Apostles. That's why since the very beginning of gospel proclamation, we have been commanded to love each other.

Love's Absence is Hatred Leading to Death (3:12-15)

Over two thousand years ago, Jesus took a group of disciples to a ridge of hills northwest of Capernaum. From this vantage point, His hearers would have a magnificent view of the Sea of Galilee. This, of course, is the site of what is probably Jesus' most famous discourse, referred to as the Sermon on the Mount. I imagine his disciples were very eager to hear what he had to say. I also imagine the stunned looks on their faces as He began to teach them about hatred and murder. Pointing back to the Old Covenant, Jesus reminded them of what they had heard over and over again, "Do not murder." But as with many things, Jesus upped the standard. Jesus even taught in Matthew 5:22 that everyone angry with others would be subject to the same judgment as a murderer. That was a strong statement. Jesus views the judgment for murder the same as the hatred and anger that led to the murder.

John will do the same thing in this set of verses. First, He begins by providing an example of hatred towards your brethren that all would know of: Cain. Cain was an ultimate example of hatred because he murdered his brother. For most of you, I don't need to reiterate the story of Cain and Abel. It's a story literally as old as time itself. But what makes the example of Cain key to understanding this passage of 1 John is this: Cain presented himself outwardly as a God-worshiper. Even though he presented himself as a worshiper, even bringing an offering to God, he was evil at heart. As one commentary puts it, "Cain's actions revealed his true spiritual father, the Devil."[2] After all, this is what Jesus says the Devil was from the beginning: a murderer. The Greek word translated as "murderer" in verse 12 is a

---

[2] Daniel L. Akin, *Christ-Centered Exposition: Exalting Jesus in 1, 2, and 3 John*, eds. David Platt, Daniel L. Akin, and Tony Merida (Nashville, TN: B&H Publishing Group, 2014), 76

particularly gruesome word. It means to slay, slaughter, butcher, or be put to death by violence.

Why would Cain do this? What could lead to such reckless actions against one's own brother? John says in verse 12 that it was "because his works were evil, and his brother's were righteous." What an interesting answer. Cain hated his brother because Abel was righteous. Cain was evil. That's why his offering wasn't accepted and Abel's was. Abel brought the right offering with the right heart. Cain brought an evil offering (some of his produce instead of the best) with an evil heart.

John then brings an application in verse 13. If Cain hated Abel because he was righteous, then the world will hate those who follow Jesus for the same reason. The world will treat the saints like Cain treated Abel. Why? Because God's children have been made righteous by the blood of Christ. Cain was evil and hated the righteousness of Abel. In hating righteousness, he hated the God who had gifted it to Abel. It is the same with believers in this world. The system of the world is at odds with the imputed righteousness given to those who have trusted Christ for salvation. Believer, the very gift God has given you to justify you and make you right before Him is the very thing the world hates about you. Through faith you have been made right with God, but you have been put at odds with the world.

So how are we to respond to the world's hate? John says we act as those who "have passed from death to life." In other words, we don't bend to the level of hate that the world does. We don't return hatred with hatred. Don't be like Cain. The gospel has changed you. God has given you a new heart. He has replaced all the hatred with love for each other. As a matter of fact, John says that this love is the evidence that we have passed from death to life. Hatred for the brothers and sisters in Christ exposes a heart that is still dead in sin. It has not been changed. These are harsh words from John. An absence of love is hatred that leads to death.

In John's day, and in ours, there are people in the church who hate the church. They are like Cain. They profess to be part of the church. They claim to be God-worshippers. But they hate God's Bride. How can this be? It is because they are not born again. They are still spiritually dead. Someone whose life is characterized and dominated by hate has not experienced the new birth. You have to appreciate John's candor here. There is no middle ground. You either love the saints or you don't. And if you don't, you are not one.

John goes even further in verse 15 in his comparison with those who hate the church to Cain. Not only are they like him in their hatred, they are also a murderer. This is where Jesus' teaching on the Sermon on the Mount becomes vital to interpreting this verse. John was there that day on those hills overlooking the Sea of Galilee. He heard Jesus' words first hand. He may have even been as stunned as everyone else. Jesus wasn't just expounding on the law that day; He was speaking as one who has authority over it. He spoke as one who was the Author of the Law. Jesus drew a line in the sand that day. It wasn't just the physical act of murder to which God was opposed. He stood opposed to, and would bring judgment against, the heart of hatred that leads to the act of murder. Hatred for the church devalues life as much as actual murder, according to John. This is a real heart check for those in John's day who were trying to rip the church apart with their hatred and false teachings. False teachings about Jesus, after all, was one of the ways this hatred for the church was manifesting itself. Someone who would intentionally lead the church down the path of false doctrine hates the church. False doctrine is murder to the church. Without the correct teaching about Jesus and salvation, the church is dead in sin. To teach something false to the church about Jesus is the same as saying to the church, "I hate you." A person who would do that, according to John in verse 15, has no eternal life.

Oh brothers and sisters, I hope we see how seriously God takes love for each other. I hope we see how seriously he takes purity of doctrine. The truth of the word of God is the very life of the church. Without it we would all be dead in trespasses and sin. May we never allow our love for each other to falter by promoting hatred and false doctrine among ourselves. May we desire to be conformed to the image of Jesus more and more every day. May we live truth as love in action. That is what John turns to next in verses 16-18.

Love's Evidence is Sacrificial Living (3:16-18)

According to John, there is a very definitive test that reveals whether someone has come to truly know love: the test of sacrifice and suffering. Christian love is distinguishable in the world because it is self-sacrificing. The world measures status by what you acquire. The kingdom of God measures status by what you are willing to give away.

Of course, Jesus is the ultimate example of this selfless, sacrificial love. In laying His life down, He set a standard for us as His people. He also taught this during His earthly ministry. He called for those who would follow Him to deny themselves and take up their cross. (Mark 8:34). He also said that the greatest love is he who would lay down his life for his friend. He didn't just teach self-sacrifice; He demonstrated it on the cross. No one took

Jesus' life from Him. He freely laid it down. We might be offended when we hear Jesus calling for us to lay our own lives down if He hadn't been willing to do the same. But He did. He doesn't just call for us to suffer; He suffers with us. He doesn't just call for us to deny ourselves; He denied Himself first. Jesus can call for us to be willing to die because He was and did.

This kind of sacrificial love is ultimately demonstrated by a willingness to die, but it also has many more practical and everyday implications as well. John gives us an example in verse 17. A person who loves the way Jesus did would never see his brother or sister in need and turn a blind eye to them. To do that means that the love of Christ was not in you. One author puts it this way, "John knows that our hearts control our hands. A closed heart will always result in closed hands and is evidence that your heart has never been opened by the 'key of the gospel' of God's grace poured out in Jesus."[3]

James would say the same thing, but in a different way. In James 2:15-17, it says, "If a brother or sister is poorly clothed and lacking in daily food, and one of you says to them 'go in peace, be warmed and filled,' without giving them the things needed for the body, what good is that? So also faith by itself, if it does not have works, is dead," (ESV).

To sum up these verses from 1 John 3, there are two types of sacrifice required of those who truly love Jesus and follow his example: the sacrifice of dying and the sacrifice of giving. One sacrifice requires us to lay down our lives for the sake of the gospel and our brothers and sisters. It is a noble thing to be willing to die to make Christ known. It is a worthy cause to give your life in service to the church and the message of the gospel. But to say you are willing to die means nothing if you aren't also willing to sacrifice

---

[3] Akin, *Christ-Centered Exposition*, 79

by giving all you have for the ministry of the gospel. What good is it to tell someone you love them enough to die for them, but you turn a blind eye to their needs and suffering? If you know of a brother who has no heat in the winter because he can't pay his electric bill, and you have the means to help him but don't, then John would say that the love of Jesus is not truly in you, no matter what you may say. If a widow in your church is suffering from loneliness and you are not willing to sacrifice time to fellowship with her, then John would likewise say that the love of Jesus is not evident in your life.

The first question of, "Are you willing to lay down your life?" is followed by, "Will you demonstrate that willingness by sacrificial living?" Will you devote your life and your resources to making the gospel known and serving the saints?

I will conclude this chapter with a brief story of someone I met in 2019 who embodies this sacrificial spirit. His name is Pastor Santa. I can't tell you exactly where he lives and ministers because he ministers in a country strongly opposed to the work of the gospel. The predominant religions in his country of origin were mainly Buddhism and Hinduism. At the age of twelve, Santa heard the gospel and was saved by the grace of God. His family was so distraught with his conversion that he was forced to leave home at the age of fourteen. At the age when many of us are still so utterly dependent on our parents' care, he was on his own. To his family, he had turned his back on his ancestors. But Santa had gained a new family in Christ. He could have given up, but he kept pursuing the faith. I honestly don't know much of Santa's story, but I do know that it would take an immense amount of sacrifice to leave everything you had once known behind to follow Jesus. That is what he did.

The results of his ministry are amazing. By his mid-thirties, he had participated in planting over 100 churches in South Asia. He had led many to Christ personally and had discipled many. He is passionate about the gospel. He knows what it costs to follow Christ in that culture, and he is willing to endure it and to call others to endure it. I met Santa on the same trek to hard-to-reach villages in South Asia I mentioned earlier in this chapter. He was our primary guide. One of the places we trekked to was his home village. See, they had kicked him out, but he didn't give up on them. Twenty years ago he was forced to leave. Now there was a church there and a small, but thriving, Christian community. This community included his own parents, whom I met and prayed for. Santa was willing to give up everything and God used the testimony of his sacrifice to lead his village to Christ.

This is what John meant in verse 18 when he said, "Let us not love in word or talk but in deed and truth." True love is truth in action. Live what you believe. In uncertain times, it isn't enough to just say what you believe; you must demonstrate it. You must live a radically sacrificial life. Living the gospel means being willing to suffer and die, but it also means having open hands and hearts for those around you. Hatred characterizes the world. Radical self-sacrificing love should characterize the follower of Jesus. Jesus, after all, didn't just speak truth; He lived it.

Chapter 8| The Live-Giving Benefits of Love

1 John 3:19-24

The human heart is a complicated organ. I'm not just talking biologically. I'm talking emotionally and spiritually as well. Many great theologians have written about the heart, but no man truly understands it.

The Greek word used for heart in the passage we will look at in this chapter is used over one hundred sixty times in the Bible. It is the word *kardia*. This word was often used to refer to the center of all physical and spiritual life. The heart was seen as the fountain and seat of a person's thoughts, passions, desires, appetites, and affections. In English, this word has also been translated as "soul" or "conscience." To put it plainly, the *kardia* is the fount from which everything about us flows. It is our inmost being. It is who we are at our core.

The human heart is complex and vulnerable, but it is a vital part of who we are. Jesus famously said in Matthew 12:34, "The mouth speaks from the overflow of the heart." We have a hard time hiding what is really in our hearts. The heart helps us make moral choices. It allows us to express emotions. We have even developed sayings and platitudes such as "follow your heart" or "the heart doesn't lie". The problem is that the human heart has been affected by sin. It can often lead us astray or confuse us. Jeremiah 17:9 says, "The heart is more deceitful than anything else, and incurable—who can understand it?"

For believers, our hearts often suffer from doubt or worry. We self-condemn and feel inadequate. This can cause us to have setbacks in our walk with Christ, and even, in extreme cases, it can lead some to doubt their salvation. But there is good news for the afflicted heart. God knows all and God sees all. God's Word and His Spirit offer us assurances as His children. God, through love, gives us life. This chapter examines three aspects of the life-giving benefits of God's love to the restless human heart.

Love Assures Us of Our Salvation (3:19-20)

John makes it clear in these two verses that we can have assurance that we "belong to the truth," (1 John 3:18). As we discussed in the previous chapter, a believer's love is manifested in truth and action. Truth is meant to be lived out. What you truly believe in your heart will manifest itself in your daily actions and speech. A person who lives a lifestyle of love demonstrates that he belongs to the truth. Love in action is one of the truest tests of a person's heart.

Living a lifestyle of love is hard work, though. It requires self-sacrifice and self-denial. It also requires that we be willing to serve others and give generously of our time and resources. How much are you willing to serve your brothers and sisters in Christ? One commentary talks about the daunting task of serving this way by saying, "In some ways we would prefer to hear Jesus' call to deny father and mother, houses and land for the sake of the gospel than his word to wash feet."[1] The truth of radical self-denial makes us feel like we are accomplishing something kingdom worthy. It's commendable. It's sacrificial. Don't get me wrong, we need people in the church willing to forsake all for the sake of the gospel. But washing feet isn't as glamorous. It isn't as noteworthy or commendable. But it is also what we are called to do for one another.

Service means always putting others before yourself. It sometimes means doing the ordinary or mundane or the trivial. Doing this kind of service is of great benefit to the kingdom, but you may never have a building or a street or an honorary Baptist offering named after you. But every act of self-denial is recorded by your Savior in the Lamb's book of life. It is noted with an asterisk by Christ. When you do things that people on earth will never notice, God notices. And the God who sees your secret deeds will reward you one day.

Service requires love and humility. When we serve in humility, our hearts are assured that we belong to God. But our hearts are still fickle organs. Even in the midst of selfless service, our hearts can still be afflicted by doubt. But John in verse 20 says not to worry. Even if our hearts still condemn us, God is greater than our fickle, afflicted hearts. God knows who you truly are. Not only does he know us, he desires for us to have assurance. He delights in it. Those who have trusted Christ alone for salvation have no reason to fear condemnation. In Romans 8:1, Paul reminds us that "therefore, no condemnation now exists for those in Christ Jesus."

Sometimes we may have a guilty conscience, but God does not want that for you. Our hearts can often be like someone giving us a guilt trip. It

---

[1] Daniel L. Akin, *Christ-Centered Exposition: Exalting Jesus in 1, 2, and 3 John*, eds. David Platt, Daniel L. Akin, and Tony Merida (Nashville, TN: B&H Publishing Group, 2014), 83

reminds us of past sins and struggles. Our heart has a memory that rarely fails. Sometimes past habits and sinful emotions can seem to come from nowhere, and this troubles us. This is where God's truth and his promises come in. Even when our hearts attempt to convince us we are guilty, God's word reminds us that Christ died as propitiation for our sins and stands even now as our Advocate. Christian, God knows all things, and He is greater than our hearts.

This doesn't mean that our hearts lie to us all the time. If you are in Christ, then He is in you. He gave you the Holy Spirit to guide you, teach you, and convict you. If you have a guilty conscience because of sin, your heart, rightly convicted by God, can lead you to repentance. In other words, sometimes a guilty heart is the result of sin in our lives. God is at work in us helping us to kill sin. God in His grace is helping us daily to overcome sinful thoughts and habits.

God is at work in our hearts in both ways. He is assuring our doubting hearts that we belong to Him while at the same time calling out the sin still in our hearts and leading us to repentance. I've said it once, and I'll say it again: loving the way Jesus commands us to love is hard work. But if it is true that God is at work in us assuring our hearts of salvation, then this should also give us confidence to approach His throne in prayer.

Love Gives Us Confidence in Prayer (3:21-22)

As much as love assures us of our salvation, it also gives us great confidence in prayer. In this passage, John highlights this confidence we can have before God's throne. A *Table Talk* devotion on this passage says, "John describes the benefits of the confidence that comes once we have our hearts reassured by God. Though the shed blood of Jesus means that sin should not cause us to run from communion with God (Heb. 10:19–22; 12:1–2), we see that we will experience confidence in our prayers most fully if our hearts are reassured before Him (1 John 3:21–22). As we look to the promises of God for our salvation in the Word and trust in Him, we will grow more and more convinced that He grants His children access to His throne, leading us to approach Him boldly with our needs."[2]

What a great promise this is for us! We can approach God's throne with a clear conscience. Not only that, but we can have confidence that when we speak to God, He listens. Prayer is an amazing privilege that so many of God's children take for granted. He doesn't just desire for us to come to Him in prayer; He delights in it.

There is a problem of prayer in many of our churches. John Onwuchekwa says in his book *Prayer: How Praying Together Shapes the Church* that on any given Sunday you might see prayer present in the church assembled, "but the prayers will likely be brief and few, a couple of cursory words as musicians and speakers shuffle on and off the stage. They will likely be biblical but vague, focusing on the general promises of God for an undefined subset of people." He goes on to say "The prayers won't slow down and linger on the glories of God, his attributes, and his character. They won't meditate unhurriedly on his Word. They won't ask hearers to study their own hearts and confess specific sins. They won't ask God to help do what only he can do: save the lost, feed the hungry, liberate captives, give wisdom to world leaders, fix broken institutions, sustain persecuted Christians."[3]

---

[2] "Whatever We Ask", Ligonier, Accessed on June 10, 2020, https://www.ligonier.org/learn/devotionals/whatever-we-ask/.
[3] John Onwuchekwa, *Prayer: How Praying Together Shapes the Church* (Wheaton,

To put it plainly, we don't understand the blessing we have in prayer. If we did, we wouldn't neglect it so much. So, why don't Christians pray? There could be many reasons, but for the sake of sticking to John's argument here, he says even a guilty or doubting conscience can lead to a less vibrant prayer life. In other words, we don't tend to call on God when we are carrying the burden of a condemning conscience. But this is the beautiful thing about the love John is talking about: We can rest in the fact that God loves us. If we are His, we no longer stand condemned before Him.

Have you ever heard someone say something like, "I know God has forgiven me, but I can't forgive myself?" This is self-condemnation. We are our own worst critics and our harshest judge sometimes. John points us to the truth of who God is and who He says we are. He is greater than our conscience! He knows us better than we know ourselves! And if God can forgive us, we ought to rest in that truth and forgive ourselves. In the words of John MacArthur, "Love banishes self-condemnation."[4]

When we recognize this truth, it frees us to love more deeply and serve more joyfully. It also leads us to pray more confidently. God hears you. His grace is louder than the voices of condemnation in your own head. We can pray with a clear conscience before God. Prayer is one way we demonstrate our submissiveness to God. In it, He aligns our wills with His. We are no longer selfish in our prayer life, but selfless. We can ask things of God from a heart that trusts Him to answer according to His will. This doesn't mean God gives us everything we want, but it does mean that in prayer we are learning to trust His character and provision. As He reveals himself to us in His word and through prayer, we learn to love Him more

---

IL: Crossway, 2018), 13-14
[4] John MacArthur, *The MacArthur Bible Commentary* (Nashville, TN: Thomas Nelson, 2005), 1962

deeply. We then ask for things in alignment with His revealed will and trust Him to answer according to His character. Prayer is indeed love in action. It is actively placing our lives in the hands of our heavenly Father who loves us, and we can have confidence He hears.

Love Assures Us of Salvation (3:23-24)

The greatest benefit of God's love for us is that He has chosen to abide in us. In these verses, John sums up what it is God commands us to do, and in following those commands He reminds us that He will remain in us through His spirit.

Verse 23 uses a version of the word "command" three times. This verse acts as a summary of all things John has been teaching up until this point. There are two primary commands God has given us: to believe in the name of his Son and to love one another. Let's first examine the phrase "believe in the name of His Son Jesus Christ," (1 John 3:23). When you break that command down it is telling us exactly what it is about His Son that God is commanding us to believe.

First, He commands us to believe on His name. Jesus' name means "Yahweh saves" or "Yahweh is salvation." Jesus name in Aramaic was *Yeshua*, the same word from which we derive the name Joshua. So, to believe in the name of Jesus means we believe He was the one sent by God to save. He is the one who brings salvation. Jesus' name conveys the truth of His identity, His work, and what His life, death, and resurrection accomplished. To speak the name of Jesus is to proclaim God saves, and He is our salvation. God's plan of salvation wasn't a new set of rules or another fallible human king or leader. His plan was to incarnate and become flesh.

His plan was a perfect person, fully God and fully man, and His name is Jesus.

Secondly, we are commanded to believe Jesus is the Son, the second member of the Trinity. Jesus was unique in his relationship with the Father. In being the Son, that means He is the eternally-existing Son. He is the eternal word, the *logos*, of John 1:1, "In the beginning was the word, and the word was with God, and the word was God." We are also commanded to believe Jesus was the Christ, the anointed one of God. He was the long-awaited and foretold Messiah of the Old Testament. He was the seed of Abraham that would bless the nations. He was the King in the line of David who would rule forever, the suffering servant of Isaiah, and the initiator of the new covenant in Jeremiah.

When you put all this together you see that we are commanded to believe all Jesus says He is: God's salvation, God's Son, and the anointed Messiah. Any gospel message that doesn't proclaim the totality of who Jesus is, quite frankly, is a false gospel. We are to trust all of Him. Belief in only one aspect of Jesus' identity *is* unbelief.

For those who obey the command to believe, God makes them a promise. We see this promise in verse 24 when John says, "The one who keeps His commands remains in Him, and He in them." God Himself remains in those who remain in the truth of Jesus. This is a gracious gift of God. The keeping of God's commands can never be separated from abiding in God. You can't obey if He is not abiding in you. God's love for us makes love for Him and obedience to His commands possible. His Spirit daily reassures our hearts that we belong to Him. The abiding of His Spirit in us is a gift of His grace. His Spirit in us helps us discern what is true from the anti-Christ spirits in the world. The Spirit is our guide, teacher, and assurance. He is the down payment for our eternal inheritance. He convicts us of sin and indwells us with righteousness.

The truth of God's abiding presence in us daily reminds us of His unfailing love for us. We belong to Him, and He belongs to us. We are His children, and He is our father. He invites us to pray to Him. He delights in hearing our voice. He takes joy in reassuring our hearts of His mercy and grace towards us. He desires to heal our condemning consciences and to affirm us as His children through the abiding presence of His Spirit in us. What a glorious truth to hold on to when times are so uncertain.

Chapter 9| Standing Firm in the Truth
1 John 4:1-6

I.   We Test Every Spirit (v.1)

II.   We Affirm a Better Confession (v.2-3)

III.   We Trust a Greater Spirit (v.4-6)

It was unlike anything I had ever seen or experienced. I had always believed in the reality of the spiritual realm. The Bible is clear: Satan is real and demons exist. Spiritual warfare is all around us. But I had never in my life experienced this reality more than in 2019 on a trip to South Asia.

I have mentioned other aspects of this trip in previous chapters. It was a wonderful, spiritually-exhilarating experience overall. A team of fourteen total had spent seven days trekking some of the most beautiful and steep mountains sharing the gospel village to village. The people we encountered were precious. Even though they had very little as far as material possessions, they were very welcoming to us and treated us as honored guests. But the whole time, you could sense a lostness among the people. We would enter their homes and see idols on shelves or adorning their bodies as jewelry. The light of the gospel was definitely needed in this place.

When that trek was over, we rejoiced in the work God had done. Almost five hundred people came to know the Lord. Many Christian groups and churches have been planted since then. We had a meal to celebrate when we returned back to the main city from which we had started. The following day we returned to the home of the missionary we were working with on the trip. We were informed that the next day we were going to go tour two of the most famous religious sites in this particular country. One of these sites was a Hindu temple.

The day arrived, and we loaded a van and drove to the temple. This was an open-air temple. You would enter the front gate and walk past many people trying to sell you small idols, trinkets, or jewelry. Inside you immediately noticed two things: First, a filthy stream that ran through the middle of it. It was built like a canal with concrete barricades on each side of the stream. At the top of the barricades were steps that lead to small platforms. I remember asking our guide, who was a Christian, what those were. He then pointed to one platform that had been very ornately decorated, and on top of it was a mound covered with a bright yellow and orange fabric. He told us that they were funeral pyres. There were bodies under the mounds of fabric. The Hindus would come there and openly burn their loved ones' bodies in the temple. Hindus believe that the body is a prison for the soul. Thus, burning the body releases the soul and frees it for its spiritual journey. The longer we were there, the more we saw bodies atop the pyres being burned. I came to find out that over one hundred bodies a day were burned at just this single temple, as Hindus believe this cremation needs to take place within twenty-four hours of death. Our guide said that every body burned there represented another lost soul who died without knowing Jesus.

Along with the pyres, I also observed that there were umbrellas sporadically placed throughout the temple, many sheltering an older male dressed in brightly-colored fabrics. Often they had on bright orange and yellow sarongs and headdresses along with bright yellow and orange painting on their foreheads. From the guide, I found out that these were Hindu priests. They were very stone-faced and solemn. When walking by them, you could almost feel the spiritual darkness that surrounded them.

Needless to say, I was overwhelmed by this spiritual experience. People were grasping for hope and comfort where none could be found. That darkness weighed heavily on me the whole visit.

It was no different in the Apostle John's day. Spiritual darkness was present and false teaching abounded. The visit to the temple reminded me of John's words in 1 John 4:1, "many false prophets have gone out into the world." The church in John's day consisted of people who had been given a false hope by a false message. They needed solid truth to stand on. That is what we will look at in this chapter as we examine how to stand firm in the truth.

We Test Every Spirit (4:1)

John begins this passage with a warning, "Do not believe every spirit." John spent a lot of time talking about the Holy Spirit in chapter three. But here he makes clear that there are other spirits at work as well. We are not to believe them all. Behind every prophetic word is a spirit. There is the Spirit of truth from God, and there is the spirit of deception from Satan. I not only think it is right, but biblical, to have a healthy skepticism regarding any teaching. We are not commanded to believe everything we hear concerning the things of God. Too much is at stake in our own spiritual lives and in the life of the church to accept every teaching that sounds godly as coming from God.

Fortunately, God has not left it up to our intellect alone to determine what is from Him and what is not. He gave us His word. John says to "test spirits to determine if they are from God," (1 John 4:1). We are commanded, not recommended, to test every spirit and every teaching regarding God, His word, and His work. But How do we test spirits? I think a great example can be found in Acts 17. Paul and Silas arrived in Thessalonica. As was his custom, Paul went to the local synagogue and began preaching the gospel. Some of the people were persuaded by Paul's message and joined him. Evidently they left the synagogue and went to the house of a man named Jason. The local Jews began to cause a ruckus and stirred up a crowd who went to Jason's home and brought him before city officials, claiming that Jason had invited men into his house who claimed a king other than Caesar. Eventually Jason was released, and later that night Jason and others sent Paul and Silas on their way for their safety.

After leaving Thessalonica, Paul and Silas went to Berea. They did the same thing here by going into the synagogue and preaching the gospel. The Bible says the people of Berea were more "open-minded than those in Thessalonica," (Acts 17:11). The Bereans welcomed the message of Christ with eagerness, but they did not believe the message just by taking Paul at his word. Acts 17:11 says they "examined the Scriptures daily to see if these things were so." They took everything Paul had just proclaimed to them about Jesus and compared it to Scripture, which at that time would have been the Old Testament. They determined that the message Paul was proclaiming lined up with what they saw in God's Word, and they believed.

This is what it means to test the spirits. This is what John called for believers in his day to do. Never take one person's word as truth unless you confirm it with God's Word. Compare what is being taught to what we know God has already revealed to us in His word. God would never send a message contrary to what He has already revealed in His Word. Test everything! That is also a command for us today. How many people have been led astray because they accepted someone's word as God's truth when it wasn't? This is important because, as John says in 1 John 4:1, "Many false prophets have gone out into the world." Along with this command comes another implied command. If we are supposed to test every spirit, then we must be deeply immersed in the truth of His Word. So many are led astray because they lack an elementary understanding of the gospel. We must read God's Word often and carefully and trust His Spirit to guide us and protect us from ungodly deception.

There will never be a shortage of wolves among God's sheep. The message of Christ will be attacked until the day He comes back, and we must be on guard. Anyone who claims to have a new revelation from God should be viewed with skepticism. There is nothing new to be added to what God has already said concerning salvation and the person and work of Christ. There will never be a new way to be saved. Only the gospel message first proclaimed by the Apostles is the true gospel. All others are counterfeits. In the words of Danny Akin, "Spiritual or religious activity is not necessarily godly activity! Watch and wait. Look and listen. Evaluate the message and the messenger by the Word of God. False prophets are deceptive in their message. And they have their own Great Commission, having been sent out 'into the world'."[1]

---

[1] Daniel L. Akin, *Christ-Centered Exposition: Exalting Jesus in 1, 2, and 3 John*

We Affirm a Better Confession (4:2-3)

There are certain aspects of the person of Jesus that cannot be denied. One of those is His incarnation. The Messiah, the Anointed One of God, came in the flesh and His name was Jesus. John makes it clear in verse 2 that one way to identify a true message from God is that it confesses the whole truth about who Jesus is.

The word "confesses" in verse 2 is the Greek word *homologeo*, which is a combination of the Greek words *homou*, meaning "same or together," and *logos*, meaning "of speech." So *homologeo* means to speak "the same as another or to assent or agree." It can also mean "to profess or to declare openly, to speak freely." What John is saying here is that the way to know if a message or person is truly of God and from God is that the person confesses the same thing as the Spirit. Namely, the person confesses the whole truth of Christ: He came in the flesh and was from God. That is the right confession about Christ.

Homologeo is used in other places in the New Testament as well. Romans 10:9 says, "If you *confess* 'Jesus is Lord', and believe in your heart that God raised him from the dead, you will be saved." 1 Timothy 6:12 says, "Fight the good fight for the faith; take hold of eternal life that you were called to and have made a good *confession* about in the presence of many witnesses." Again in Hebrews 13:15 we see this word when the author says, "Therefore, through Him let us continually offer up to God a sacrifice of praise, that is, the fruit of our lips that *confess* His name," (italics mine). John himself uses this term five times in this letter alone. In testing the

(Nashville, TN: B&H Publishing, 2014), 94

spirits, we are to give ear only to the ones that make the true and right confession about the person of Christ.

The early church did not have the totality of the New Testament to rely on like we now have. If a message is spoken in our midst, we have the New Testament to validate or invalidate the message. We can judge whether someone is confessing the truth about Christ by simply opening our Bibles. The early church had the Old Testament, but they did not have all the writings of the Apostles yet contained in one volume. What they did have were early church confessions and creeds that promoted and solidified right doctrine, particularly pertaining to the person and work of Jesus. Many of these creeds are actually recorded for us in the New Testament. Some are longer, but some are just simple phrases to teach truth. Below are a few examples:

- "He was manifested in the flesh, vindicated in the Spirit, seen by angels, preached among the nations, believed on in the world, taken up in glory"- 1 Timothy 3:16
- "...Marana tha that is , Lord come" – 1 Corinthians 16:22
- "Jesus is Lord"- recorded in Romans 10:9
- "that Christ died for our sins according to the Scriptures, that He was buried, that He was raised on the third day according to the Scriptures" - 1 Corinthians 15:3-4

Many scholars even believe that Ephesians 4:4-6 is an early church creed often spoken at the baptism of a new believer. It says, "There is one body and one Spirit-- just as you were called to one hope at your calling-- one Lord, one faith, one baptism, one God and Father of all, who is above all and through all and in all." I could also cite many other creeds and confessions, such as the Apostle's Creed of the early third century or the Nicene Creed of the fourth century. The point is that the early church relied on confessions and creeds to judge truth. In order to be from God, you must confess the right things about Christ.

It is the same for us. We must only accept right confessions about Jesus in our own lives and in the life of the church. We must hold every word up to the light of truth to see if it matches. The New Testament gives us the full revelation of who Christ is. There is no reason to accept falsehood in our midst when God has given us His word to read and His Spirit in us to guide us in truth. The reason we must be diligent about this is because there will always be the spirit of antichrists speaking falsely about Christ until He returns. This is John's warning in 1 John 4:3. He is reiterating a truth he already spoke in chapter two. The spirit of antichrist speaks lies about the person and work of Christ, he is coming, and he is already in the world now.

The real flesh and blood Antichrist may not be yet revealed, but his spirit is at work even now. The Spirit of God always honors and glorifies Christ. The spirit of antichrist defames Christ and dishonors His name. If someone says he believes in Jesus, but his doctrine of Christ does not line up with Scripture, then that person is not of Christ. Right doctrine and theology hinges on what we believe about the person of Christ. If that is wrong, it distorts and twists the rest of our theology. We must strive to be a people who embrace a right confession about Christ and pray that the Holy Spirit would help us discern and test the spirits opposed to Christ.

We Are Indwelt by a Greater Spirit (4:4-6)

I love John's response to the reality of false teaching here in these verses. He says we should not fear them. It is good and right to acknowledge the spirit of antichrist in this age. But there is no reason to fear it. Why is this? According to verse 4, we have conquered them. The Greek word translated as *conquer* here is used twenty-eight times in the New Testament. It is translated primarily as *overcome* in many places. It means "to carry off the victory, to win the case, and to maintain the cause." It is the same Greek word Jesus used in John 16:33 when He said, "I have overcome the world."

We as believers have rejected, and thus conquered, the false prophets and antichrists in the world. We have made the better confession: Jesus is Lord. But we haven't done this in our own power. John makes it clear that we have overcome because "the One who is in you is greater than the one who is in the world." Who is this one? God's very Spirit that abides in you. He is greater. The Holy Spirit dwells in each believer and is a built-in alarm for false teaching. False teachers are wise, but He is wiser. False teaching is alluring, but He is more so. False teaching claims to satisfy, but only He truly satisfies. We must trust the Holy Spirit in us because only He gives us the power to overcome the world and to discern the cacophony of false messages around us daily.

John gives God's people a reminder in verse 5: Those who come bearing falsehoods about the person and work of Christ are from the world. We defined "world" earlier in this book by saying that it refers to the system of the world that stands opposed to God's word, ways, and people. People who come from the world bear the message of the world. And that message is one that, even if it sounds good and pleasing, is opposed to God. When the messengers of the world speak, the people of the world listen. We shouldn't be surprised the world would listen to and embrace the message of false teachers. Lost people act lost and live lost. They don't know Christ. His Word and His Spirit are not in them. This is a warning for all believers. Anytime someone claiming to come from God speaks a message that is wholeheartedly embraced by the world, that should alarm us. The church of the Lord Jesus ought not embrace a message with which the world has no problem. The cross and the gospel offend. The message of Jesus will always be at odds with the world.

This is also a warning to preachers: If the world applauds your message, you are walking a dangerous road. As a proclaimer of the gospel, who would you rather be at odds with: the world or God? Who would you rather be embraced by: the world or God? Who will stand as the final judge to your faithfulness in proclaiming the whole counsel of the Word: the world or God? If you are a believer, and especially if you are a pastor, you ought to fear not him who can only destroy the body but fear Him who can also destroy both body and soul in hell (Matthew 10:28).

Eternity is at stake. Souls are at stake. The offense of the cross must be proclaimed. We are, after all, as John puts it in 1 John 4:6, "from God." We are those who know God. Those who have confessed Christ as Lord listen to those truly sent from God. John, as an apostle, recognized that those who truly belonged to God embraced his message about Christ. This is how simple it is to discern the "Spirit of truth and the spirit of deception," (1 John 4:6). Those who embrace the message of the Apostles as laid out in the New Testament are of God; those who reject the message of the Apostles are not.

This is why expository, biblical preaching is so important to the life of a church. It is where the church as a body assembles to hear the message of the Apostles and the Word of God proclaimed weekly. One of the main reasons we ought not to forsake the assembling together of God's people is that we need to hear God's Word rightly proclaimed often. Those who are faithful to a church where God's truth is rightly expounded upon will be less likely to be led astray by the spirit of deception. Those who forsake the assembly are easier targets for the antichrists of this world. The spirit of deception is very active, and God's people must be on guard at all times.

To stand firm in the truth in uncertain times, we must test every spirit, we must embrace and teach the right confession about Christ, and we must trust the greater Spirit in us. We look forward to the day when all false teaching and spirits of antichrist will be silenced and defeated once and for all. We must confess He came in the flesh. We must confess He lived a perfect and sinless life. We must confess He died as our substitute on the cross to pay for our sins. We must confess He was laid in a tomb but three days later rose claiming victory over sin and death. We must confess that He has ascended back to heaven and even now is at the right hand of God interceding for the saints. We must confess that He will return in power and glory with his Bride, the Church. We must confess that at that moment all will be made new, death and sin will vanish forever, and we will reign eternally with our King forever and ever, Amen.

Chapter 10| Celebrate Jesus, True Love Incarnate
1 John 4:7-19

I.   True Love's Origin (v.7-8)

II.   True Love's Revelation (v.9)

III.   True Love's Demonstration (v.10-12)

IV.   True Love's Implications (v.13-19)

One could say that this passage from 1 John is the pinnacle of his teaching on love. Of all the things John says regarding love in the life of the believer, none of them are more important than the simple phrase: God is love. He is love incarnate.

We often use the word incarnate or incarnation at Christmastime. It is, after all, what the whole season is about. A time to reflect on, celebrate, and stand in awe and wonder at the incarnation of the Son. Defined, incarnate means "to be made manifest or comprehensible." It can also mean "to be invested with bodily or human form." As it relates to Jesus, when we use the word incarnate or incarnation, we are speaking about Him being the fleshly embodiment of deity in earthly form. The person of Christ unifies divinity and humanity.

The passage we are looking at in this chapter also says that God is love. He is the manifestation of love. So if God is love, and Jesus is God, then Jesus is love made flesh-- love incarnate. The predominate Greek word for love in the New Testament is *agapao* which transliterated is *agape*. It is used twenty-one times in these thirteen verses of 1 John. It can be translated as love, affection, or benevolence. The word itself is simple, but the emotion and context behind the word is very deep. That's what we will look at in this chapter. How is love defined in this passage, and what are love's implications for us?

True Love's Origin (4:7-8)

John begins here with a command to love one another. This isn't arbitrary. Love is a defining characteristic of a believer. John would say it is *the* characteristic of a believer. To love is divine; it's godly. It is to display to others the chief attribute of God's character.

John then spells out that the origin of love is God himself. This is interesting, because love isn't man-made. It didn't originate in our hearts. We often define love in terms of just pure sentiment or in sexual terms. Here John says that love has a divine origin. It comes from God, who is love. What does this mean? John Piper says it well when he says, "Love is from God the way heat is from fire, or the way light is from the sun. Love belongs to God's nature. It's woven into what He is. It's part of what it means to be God. The sun gives light because it is light. And fire gives heat because it is heat." [1]

---

[1] John Piper, "The New Birth Produces Love", Desiring God, Published March 16, 2008, https://www.desiringgod.org/messages/the-new-birth-produces-love

Verse 7 also makes it clear that that in order to truly love, one must be born of God. Love is the chief evidence that you know God and have been born again. To be born again is to be changed from the inside out by the power of God. His Spirit does a work in your heart, enabling a new kind of love. This is a self-sacrificing type of love that elevates others above you. It is a love that views God as its supreme joy and affection, and a love that can only come from God. This is a radical love the world doesn't understand. It's the kind of love that never says, "I don't love you anymore." It's the kind of love that never lets go, and it never leaves. It's the kind of love that doesn't merely invite the lost to come to church but invites them to experience Christ.

This radical type of love is such a distinguishing characteristic of a true believer that in 1 John 4:8 John goes so far as to say that if someone doesn't exhibit this type of love, then they do not know God. Love is not just an emotion that comes and goes; it is a habit daily displayed in our words and actions. If God is love, then those who have been born of God and know God display that they are connected to love's source, which is God Himself.

True Love's Revelation (4:9)

John says that the only way we can come to know the radical, self-sacrificing love of God is for Him to reveal it to us. This is a theme in all of Scripture. God can't be found by human means. He must be revealed by divine ones. God isn't discovered; He makes Himself known. So it is with His love.

The word *revealed* here in verse 9 can also be translated as "manifested." It means to make known, to be made visible, or to be made clear or put on display. The primary way God has revealed His love to us is through the sending of His Son. Jesus is the means by which the essence of God's love for us is made visible. In Christ, God has put His love on display.

Hebrews 1:3 says, the Son is the "radiance of God's glory and the exact expression of His nature…" Christ was the final and fullest revelation of God. He radiated the glory of the Father and was by His very nature God. Have you ever looked at a little boy and said, "He looks and acts exactly like his Dad"? A father usually swells up with pride at hearing that comment. Jesus was just like His Father, and His Father delighted in Him.

Christ was the *only* Son of God. Some translations use the word begotten. He was the unique Son.

True Love's Demonstration (4:10-12)

There are two things we must always keep in mind when we talk about the first advent of Christ. First, it is a time of celebration of His first coming. At the same time, we are also to look and wait expectantly for His second coming. But it's the purpose for the first coming that should dominate our view of the Nativity.

John says three very important phrases in verse 4:10. First, he says, "Not that we loved God." God's love for us wasn't prompted by our love for Him. He didn't see us longing for Him or reaching out in love for Him and then decide to love us in response. Our sinful hearts were not capable of the kind of love God has. The Bible says that before salvation we had no love for God; we were enemies of God, and haters of righteousness who prefer the dark to light. We did not love first.

This is the second truth of 1 John 4:10, "He loved us." God's love pre-empted ours. His love enabled ours. He is love, and He loved us first. Not only that, but His love led Him to do something so wild, so drastic, and so magnificent to redeem us that we never would have imagined it. This is the third truth: He "sent His Son to be the propitiation for our sins," (1 John 4:10).

You see, standing like a dark, looming shadow over the manger is the cross. Christ was the love of God made flesh. And the greatest demonstration of that love was when the Son offered himself on the cross as payment for our sins. He was taking our curse. He was our shield against the wrath of God. He took it all on Himself. This wasn't an afterthought of God; it was His plan. He sent His Son, born of a virgin, for the purpose of being our propitiation and our atonement. That babe in a manger would grow up to be the God-man who embraces his destiny as the Crucified-Savior and Redeemer of sinful man. The wonder of the incarnation gave way to the horror of the cross which will gave way to the glory of the resurrection.

This is a very radical love God has for us. Second Corinthians 5:19 says it this way: "In Christ, God was reconciling the world to Himself, not counting their trespasses against them." If God loves us in this way, "we also must love one another," (1 John 4:11). Christmas is a time to not only reflect on the great love of God demonstrated in sending His Son, but it's a time to renew our commitment to display the love of God to each other. See, God's love was a very self-sacrificing type of love. What time is better than Christmas to ask God to once again stir your affections for your brothers and sisters in Christ, for the lost and dying of the world, and for the least of these all around us?

God's love is not only our example but the motivating factor behind our love for each other. You were in darkness, and God sent the Light. You were dead in trespasses and sin, and God gave life. You were a slave to sin, and God, in mercy, paid the price for your freedom. You were His enemy, and through Christ you are now adopted as family and a co-heir. What more motivation do we need to love as we ought? Our love for others is essentially a response of gratitude for God's love for us.

In verse 12, John makes a very distinct point about the church, and all of us should pay attention here. The love of God, great as it is, is invisible. No one has seen God. But when we love each other as we ought and when we practice *agapao*, it is proof that God is indeed among us and that His love is real. We are the only visible demonstration of God's love this lost world sees. In us, God's love is perfected or brought to completion.

God's love is active. It's not pure emotion, but it is actually accomplishing something. True love doesn't just stir our hearts; it changes people. It transforms them. You don't believe that? Go find someone who has never really been loved. Go find someone who has been neglected. The absence of this kind of love in a person's life is devastating. God's kind of love, exhibited in His church and in our love for each other, is accomplishing something. It is changing hearts and restoring lives.

The negative aspect of this love should shake us to our core. When we fail to love as we ought, we are telling a lost and dying world something false about the love of God. The purpose of God's love at work in you is so that you might love others as God loves.

So there is some deep truth about love, *agapao*, we find in these six verses. We learn that true love originates with God and is the very essence of His being. We learned that God's greatest revelation of His love was the sending of His Son to be our propitiation. Because of this, we can experience the love of God, and in turn we display that love to each other as a witness to the world of the great love of God. From this, John gives us three personal implications or conclusions we can draw from this.

True Love's Implications (4:13-19)

The first of these implications comes from 1 John 4:13-16, which assures us of our salvation. When you love as God loves, this is evidence in your life that you have His Spirit and that He abides in you. To love as God loves requires the power of God. The fact that this love abides in us is our assurance of salvation. Loving this way means He is with you. And if He is with you, you are His and belong to Him. A major part of the Spirit's work in our life is to provide constant assurance that we do indeed belong to God.

In 4:14-15 John re-affirms what he has already been saying to the churches in this letter, namely, that he was an eyewitness to the fact that Christ was really the Son sent by God to be the Messiah and Savior of the world. He saw it first-hand. He witnessed the miracles of Jesus. He heard Jesus teaching with his own ear. John was at the foot of the cross as Jesus bled and died, was witness to the empty tomb, spent time with the resurrected Christ, and stood gazing as Christ ascended into heaven. He was there at Pentecost when God's Spirit, like a mighty rushing wind, filled His people and transformed them from scared former disciples into bold, gospel-preaching apostles.

John was a witness to the fact that if any "confesses that Jesus is the Son of God-- that God would come and remain in him and he in God," (1 John 4:15). He had seen the rich and the poor come to Christ, and he had seen God's Spirit change leaders and politicians as well as farmers and carpenters. John's life mission was to take the good news to the world: A Savior was born in Bethlehem, He died on a cross as atonement for His people, and He was resurrected from the dead. Anybody who would hear that message, receive that message, and confess Jesus as Lord would receive the Holy Spirit as assurance.

God abides in those who confess Christ. If you are a believer today, you also have come to know and believe the love God has for us in Christ. You know this because His love is in you, and it will remain in you because you are His. The Holy Spirit reminds us that our salvation is a settled issue in our hearts. God's love in you doesn't stir up doubt about your salvation, but it reassures with hope and love that you are His.

One of the most interesting phrases John uses in this passage is in verse 16 when he tells the church to "remain in the love of God." As a believer, the love of God for me is a settled truth in my heart, but I am also commanded to abide in it. If God does indeed abide in us, then we will abide, or remain, in Him. To abide in Him means that we let the truth of the gospel so settle in our hearts that we will not be moved to doubt or insecurity regarding our salvation. These truths settle in our hearts through prayer, Bible study, fellowshipping with the saints, partaking of the Lord's Supper, etc. To fail to abide in Him doesn't mean He leaves you; it just means you become susceptible to falling into doubt and insecurity. Therefore, abide in the love of God, as He abides in you, and allow His love to reassure you daily that you belong to Him.

The second implication comes from 1 John 4:17. We can be confident in the day of judgment. John is speaking about how we should view the day of judgment. We should view it both positively and negatively.

In other words, because of God's great love we can be confident (positive) in regards to the day of judgment, and not fear it (negative) at the same time. Let's first address our confidence.

This seems like an odd statement. Many encounters with God are recorded both in the Old Testament and the New Testament. All of these encounters involve men getting a glimpse of God and becoming terrified. The judgment of God is very real. It will happen. Just as surely as the sun will rise tomorrow, Christ will return, and judgement will happen. Jesus spoke forcefully and often about the day of judgment. When you think about it, the purpose of spreading the gospel is so that people may be made right with God and thus be prepared for that day. John says not only can we be prepared, but we can be confident. Why?

John says, "For we are as He is in this world," (1 John 4:17). What does he mean by that? The best I can surmise is that if you are in Christ, if you are abiding in the love of God and He is abiding in you, then you stand in relation to God in the same way Christ does. God treats us in the same way as His Son. John MacArthur says it this way, "If Jesus called God Father, so may we, since we are accepted in the Beloved (Eph. 1:6)."[2] 1 John 3:2b says, "We know that when He appears, we will be like Him because we will see Him as He is." On that day, we will finally understand that Christ is enough. Before God, He will not see us as we too often see ourselves-- as this sinful, undeserving, often falling short, and prone to wander person. He will lavish on us a welcome as His very own sons and daughters. He will remove our filthy rags and give us pure white robes. Mortality will be exchanged for immortality and corruption for incorruption. We can be

---

[2] John MacArthur, *The MacArthur Bible Commentary* (Nashville, TN: Thomas Nelson,2005), 1965

confident in this. The deep *agapao* love of God makes this confidence possible.

The third implication from this text is that we can have fearlessness in life (1 John 4:18-19). God's love gives us confidence as we await the day of judgement. The same *agapeo* love that builds our confidence in light of judgment also banishes fear from our daily lives.

Let's first discuss what this isn't talking about in relation to fear. This passage isn't talking about natural fears, such as not petting bears or swimming with sharks or walking up on a pack of wolves. We also have other fears like playing with a brown recluse spider, kissing someone with the flu, and sky diving without a parachute. It's good to fear those things. Your life depends on that type of fear.

The idea of fear in this passage also does not refer to a healthy fear of the Lord. This is a reverential fear. It is a fear of honor. It is the same type of fear a child might have for his or her parents. Proverbs says that this type of fear of the Lord is the beginning of wisdom (Proverbs 1:7). It's the kind of fear that's healthy for a believer. It is a fear that leads us to submit to God and to be in awe of God.

What is this passage talking about? I think it means no fear of death, wrath, or final judgment. As believers, we do not have to fear being cast out by God, rejected by God at final judgment, or facing the wrath of God. Why don't we need to fear those things? Because perfect love has cast them out. It is that perfect love that is the essence of God Himself. It is that perfect love that sent His son to be born of a virgin. It is that perfect love that placed His Son on a cross to die the death we deserved, to be judged in our place, and to take on Himself the wrath of God that should have been poured out on us.

Perfect love casts out fear because perfect love has already conquered death, hell, and the grave. Perfect love casts out fear because it has already stood in our place, taken our judgment, and declared us righteous by faith in Jesus. The perfect love of Jesus overcame the grave, and He was resurrected, securing our own resurrection. When we celebrate the incarnation of Christ, we don't just look back at a Savior in a manger; we look forward to a King coming again on a white horse to gather all the redeemed from every nation. If all that is true, then what judgment is there to fear?

The origination of love is God Himself. In grace, He gave that love a face in Jesus. Jesus-- by His life, death, and resurrection-- demonstrated that love for us. In Him, we can be assured of our salvation. In Him, we can stand confidently as we await the day of judgement. In Him, we can live the life God has called us to live without fear of being rejected on that final day. The love that became incarnate in the person of Christ now lives in us, and that should lead us to a life of deeper love and obedience towards God. That is what we will discuss in the next chapter.

Chapter 11| Walk in Loving Obedience
1 John 4:20-5:5

I.   Loving God Leads to Loving Each Other (v.20-21; 5:1)

II.   Loving God Means Obeying His Word (v.2-3)

III.   Loving God Means Conquering the World (v.4-5)

In the last chapter we talked about Jesus, the incarnation of love. I had mentioned that 1 John 4 was the pinnacle of John's teaching on love. If 1 John 4:7-19 is the pinnacle of John's teaching on love, then 1 John 4:20--5:4 is the culmination of his teaching on the subject. We know that God is love. But what does it mean for us to love God? Greg Laurie, pastor of multisite church Harvest Community Fellowship in Riverside California, says that "Our love for God needs to be emotive and intelligent."[1] What he means is that we love God with our heads, our hearts, our minds, and our emotions. This sounds a lot like Moses' teaching in Deuteronomy 6:5 when he told the people to "love the Lord your God with all your heart, with all your soul, and with all your strength."

We love God best by loving Him with everything that we are. This includes, according to Moses and Jesus Himself, loving God with all our strength. We don't just love in thought or emotions only, but we also love in

---

[1] Greg Laurie, "The Key to Loving God", Harvest Church, Accessed on July 13, 2020, https://harvest.org/resources/gregs-blog/post/the-key-to-loving-god/.

deed. We love God through obedience. Eugene Peterson says, "Obedience is the thing, living in active response to the living God. The most important question we ask of this text [the Bible] is not, 'What does this mean?' but 'What can I obey?' A simple act of obedience will open up our lives to this text far more quickly than any number of Bible studies and dictionaries and concordances."[2] His point is that we learn much about God from faithful and loving obedience to His word. We demonstrate our love for God by obedience.

That is what we will discuss in this chapter. If God is love, and He displayed that love most clearly to us in the person of Jesus, then our love for Him is most clearly displayed in a life of loving obedience to our heavenly Father. There are three concrete actions that demonstrate our love for God. Let's examine them individually.

Loving God Means Loving Each Other (4:20-21; 5:1)

John here comes back to a familiar theme- love for each other. This is a clear principle in John's writing. It is impossible to say you love God with your mouth while you hate a brother or sister in Christ. To John, if you can't love a brother or sister you can see, then it is impossible to love a God you can't. If you follow John's logic here, it seems he is saying that loving someone you can't see should be harder than loving someone you can see. If a person can't possess the easier love for people he sees daily, then how can he possess the harder love for a God he can't even see?

---

[2] Eugene H. Peterson, *Eat This Book: A Conversation in the Art of Spiritual Reading* (Grand Rapids, MI: William B. Eerdman's Publishing, 2006), 71

When it comes to God, we love with the eyes of faith. By faith, we see Him as real and beautiful. We see him as glorious and majestic. By faith, we open ourselves up to the love of God, and in grace, He gives us the capacity to love Him back. And we love Him with everything we are. We love Him with all our mind when we pour over the Word He gave us. By devoting ourselves to His word, we seek a deeper understanding of who He is and what He has done for us in Christ. We love Him with all our heart when we delight in Him and take joy in Him. When we see Him as the satisfaction of all of our longings, we will glorify Him from our hearts. We love Him with all our strength when we offer our bodies up to Him as living sacrifices, denying ourselves and following Him. To love Him is to seek to know Him, cherish Him in our hearts, and to simply do what He says.

John really can't put it any simpler than he does in 1 John 4:21: To love God is to also love His people. Loving God and loving your brothers and sisters in Christ can never be separated from each other. Loving God and loving those who are His is the great *inclusio* of John's discourse on love. They are the bookends of the Christian experience: Loving God and loving His people.

This doesn't mean that we do not love those who are not saved. Certainly not! I believe the calling of the Great Commission means that we are to have such a deep love for Christ that that love overflows into a love for the lost and dying. We are to have a deep love for the hurting and the prodigals of the world. We are to go after them and share the gospel with them so that they might become a part of the family of God. We are, after all, ambassadors for Christ and messengers of reconciliation.

But there is a special familial love that believers should have for other believers. We are all part of the same body. When one part of the body mourns, we all mourn. When one part of the body rejoices, we all rejoice. So how can we identify those who are believers and who are not? John answers this in 5:1. Everyone who believes that Jesus is the Christ is born of God. That is a very simple statement, but it is very deep. Everything about the Christian experience comes back to Jesus. Everyone who is to be born of God must confess Jesus as the Messiah. Those born of God didn't just believe in Christ once upon a time: They continually believe. Our belief in Jesus as the Messiah is active; we do it daily by trusting in all of His promises for us. We haven't just trusted in Christ in the past; we also actively trust Him now daily.

We have experienced the new birth. We are new, and we are being transformed daily. To be born of God means we bear the birthmark of that transformation. We are identified with Christ and unified with His people. Those who are born of God love others who have been born of Him.

This bond goes beyond mere flesh and blood. Jesus demonstrated this in Matthew 12:46-49. As Jesus was teaching the crowds, His brothers and mother showed up wanting to speak with Him. Someone made Him aware of their request. His family, for the most part, thought Jesus was out of his mind. His brothers didn't believe in Him. His mother, I'm sure, was concerned for His safety. They wanted Him to stop teaching and come home with them. His response to hearing that His mother and brothers wanted Him was, "Who is my mother and who are my brothers?" Pointing to His disciples and His followers, He said, "Here are my mother and my brothers! For whoever does the will of my Father in heaven is my brother and sister and mother," (CSB). He wasn't rejecting His natural family, but He was prioritizing spiritual relationships with His followers and believers. We are to model that by having a deep love for our brothers and sisters who have been born again, who have been called by God, and who bear the name of Jesus.

Loving God Means Obeying His Word (5:2-3)

In addition to loving His people, we are also commanded to show our love for God and for others by obeying His word. John introduces an interesting concept here in 1 John 5:2, explaining that one of the ways we best love each other is by obeying God's commands. Our personal obedience is a display of our love for our brothers and sisters in Christ. The *ESV Study Bible* says that this is true because our love for "God's commandments shows believers the true way to do good for others. Love and law are complementary."[3] In other words, I love others best when I am practicing my love for God through obedience to his commands. Faith, love, and obedience always mutually exist with each other in Scripture. There is no mention of faith without love. There is likewise no mention of love without obedience.

Those who love God are by John's definition commandment keepers. It is also part of our mission from Christ. We are commanded to go to all the world, telling them the good news of Jesus and teaching them all things He has commanded. A key part of discipleship is teaching people all that Jesus said to do. We don't do this just so believers can know what Jesus said to do, but so that they might actually do it!

When believers start talking about obedience, a common objection might be to say that strict obedience might lead to legalism. That might be

---

[3] Robert W. Yarbrough, study notes on 1 John 5:2, in *ESV Study Bible* (Wheaton, IL: Crossway, 2008),2436

true in some sense. But obedience done in love is the opposite of legalism: It is delight. When we obey out of love for God and for others, then that obedience isn't done to earn God's favor but to display our delight in God to others.

Another objection might be, "Isn't it a burden to strive to live a life of such obedience?" Again, the answer is maybe. If you are seeking to obey in order to achieve favor with God, and you are doing so without love at the center, then, yes, that obedience will be a burden far too much to bear. But obedience built on love for God and others is no burden at all. That is what John says in 1 John 5:3: Love for God is keeping His commandments, and "His commands are not a burden." How can John say this? I can think of two reasons. First, when compared to the manmade religious traditions of the Jewish leaders, the commands of Jesus were burden-free. Jesus makes this point in Matthew 11:28-30 when he says, "Come to Me, all of you who are weary and burdened, and I will give you rest. All of you, take up My yoke and learn from Me, because I am gentle and humble in heart, and you will find rest for yourselves. For my yoke is easy and My burden is light." Jesus viewed His commands as freedom from the burden of the law and manmade religious traditions. Jesus saw a people who were asked to bear a load more than they could carry, so He invited them to come to Him and yoke up with Him so that He might take that burden on Himself and bear it for them.

Secondly, the good news of the gospel is that there is freedom from our burdens. This freedom makes loving obedience a delight. For the Christian, delight and obedience go hand in hand. God, in grace, frees us to obey him. Our response is gratitude and delight as we seek obedience to His word. Even in the Old Testament, God's law was viewed as a delight, not a burden. The Psalms are full of expressions of delight for God's law:

- "Take delight in the LORD, and He will give you your heart's desires." (Psalm 37:4)
- "I delight to do Your will, my God; Your instruction lives within me." (Psalm 40:8)
- "I will delight in Your statutes; I will not forget Your word." (Psalm 119:16)
- "Trouble and distress have overtaken me, but Your commands are my delight." (Psalm 119:143)

Our love for God and others leads to obedience, and this obedience is a delight. Love is the motivating factor. Jerry Bridges in his book *The Discipline of Grace* talks about love being the motivation behind our obedience. He says, "Love for God, then, is the only acceptable motive for obedience to Him. This love may express itself in a reverence for Him and a desire to please Him, but those expressions must spring from love. Without the motive of love, my apparent obedience may be essentially self-serving."[4]

We can't obey God's Word if we are not daily in God's Word. How can you practice obedience without a familiarity with the commands of Jesus you are supposed to be keeping? We need to daily remind ourselves of these commands. What does this practically look like? Well, for starters, you can make sure you have a daily, consistent time in God's Word. Post God's Word all over your house so you can see it often. Write it on dry erase boards. Put it on sticky notes you leave all over the house. Begin journaling

---

[4] Jerry Bridges, *The Discipline of Grace* (Colorado Springs, CO: NavPress, 2006), 114

your thoughts as you read God's Word. Do whatever it takes. Just keep God's Word before you all day. Confront yourself with truth as often as possible. And, above all else, do it out of love for God and His people.

Loving God Means Conquering the World (5:4-5)

Those who love God have been born of God. And according to John in 1 John 5:4, those born of God conquer the world. This word conquer in the Greek is *nikao*. This word is translated in other places as "overcome" or "to prevail." The meaning is simply "to be victorious over their foes" or "to carry off the victory." The picture is of a soldier winning a battle and carrying off the spoils of his victory. He has overcome and prevailed, thus all that comes with victory belongs to Him.

So it is with those who love God: We will not be compelled by the world to turn away from Christ; we have victory. The tense of the word in Greek also gives the indication that we are conquering continually. In other words, conquering the world is a daily habit for those who love God and His people. Because we are in this world, we are constantly having to wage battle against it. But because we are in Christ, we are daily and continually victorious over it. Because I am in Christ, my desire is no longer for the world, but it is for Him. For those who love God, we no longer desire the things of the world, but we desire Him. The things of this world are no longer beautiful to us because we see Him as supremely beautiful. As the old hymn, *Turn Your Eyes Upon Jesus* says, "...and the things of earth will grow strangely dim in the light of His glory and grace."[5]

---

[5] Helen H. Lemmel, "Turn Your Eyes Upon Jesus," in *The Baptist Hymnal* (Nashville, TN: Convention Press, 1991), 320

I have mentioned in other places that the phrase "the world" in Scripture usually refers to the system of the world dominated by the power of Satan. The means of overcoming the world is, according to John, our faith. By trusting in Christ and declaring Him Lord over your life, you have instantly became an overcomer. We are overcomers because by faith we are now hidden in the life, death, burial, and resurrection of the One who overcame death, hell, and the grave for us. Ultimately all those who overcome the world daily now, through faith, will one day triumphantly overcome the world once and for all at the return of Christ, when all who have trusted in Him will be raised to eternal life.

This is good news for us, but it is not good news for those still lost in sin. They are not overcomers. They are still being overcome daily by their sin and the forces of darkness. They live in a constant state of defeat, and their only hope of victory is the gospel. As overcomers, it is our responsibility and calling to tell the lost and dying that they, too, can overcome the power of sin and Satan by faith in Christ. Do we love them enough to tell them and to call them to believe in Jesus as the Son of God? We have experienced the freedom that comes with overcoming the world. Don't we want those still in bondage to experience that same freedom? Dear believers, we must love others, obey God, and daily overcome the world so that Christ may get all the glory, and so that others might come to know Him as Lord.

Chapter 12| Defend the Certain Testimony That Jesus is the Christ 1 John 5:6-12

I.   The Witness of the Water, the Blood, and the Spirit (v.6-8)

II.   The Witness of the Father and the Believer (v.9-10)

III.   The Witness of Eternal Life (v.11-12)

In July of 2019 my wife, our three kids, and I were traveling out-of-state to visit with friends. When we arrived at our destination, it was dinner time. We decided to stop and get dinner at a fast food drive-thru before heading to our hotel so we wouldn't need to get back out later. We exited off the interstate, bought our food, and were at a red light in the left turn lane waiting on the light to change. We finally got the green light. My wife, who was driving, paused to yield to oncoming traffic. When it was obvious that it was clear to turn, she made her way out into the intersection to turn left. Almost immediately we heard the squeal of tires to our left as an older model SUV locked down its brakes- barreling towards the driver's side of our minivan. My wife slammed on her brakes as well, but the crash was unavoidable. The driver slammed into the front driver's side of our vehicle at a high rate of speed, jarring us and completely tearing the front bumper off our vehicle. The other car skidded to a stop clear on the other side of the intersection.

My wife and I were shocked. If she had pulled out just a few feet more into the intersection, the SUV would have hit my wife's driver's side door head on. I checked on her, but she couldn't have cared less about herself. She was immediately checking on all the kids who were, thankfully, perfectly fine but a little shaken up. My wife, in tears, turned to me and said, "Was that my fault? Did I cause that?"

I remember saying, "No! Absolutely not. That driver ran a clear red light!"

Many people came up to our vehicle to check on us. The other driver exited his car, inspecting the damage. The cops were called as well as an ambulance. We had many concerns going through our minds at that time. We were out of state and from all appearances our vehicle had been totaled. We had no way to get to the hotel. My wife felt nauseous and her head hurt, so we agreed she needed to go to the hospital to get checked out. That left me by myself trying to figure out how to be with my wife and get my three kids to the hotel at the same time. Thankfully for us, some friends stepped in to help. I ended up going to the hotel with our shaken-up kids while a friend stayed with my wife while she was checked out at a local hospital and released soon thereafter.

That afternoon we were in need of many things: We needed an ambulance for my wife. We needed a ride to the hotel. We would eventually need to file an insurance claim and get a rental vehicle so we could get back home. But other than making sure everyone was physically okay, what we really needed at that time were witnesses. We needed people who saw the accident that could corroborate our story that the other driver had run a red light and hit our van, causing the accident. Fortunately for us, there were many witnesses. It was a crowded intersection, and everyone who spoke to the policeman making the report verified our story. We were not at fault, and we were cleared of any traffic violations, thanks to the help of eye witnesses.

It was no different in biblical times. According to the Mosaic Law, witnesses were called upon to verify the truth of a claim. We'll discuss this more later, but eye-witness testimony has always been a vital part of determining the truth of a situation.

In this passage of 1 John, the apostle is going to mention six witnesses that testify to the truth about Jesus. It's not that Jesus' testimony about himself needed corroboration. He was God in the flesh, and as God, He cannot lie. But nonetheless, we see John identify these witnesses. All of them help shed light on the person and work of Christ and verify that He was indeed the flesh and blood Son of God. For the sake of our discussion, I will group them into three groups as John discusses them in this passage.

The Witness of the Water, the Blood, and the Spirit (5:6-8)

The Water

The first group is the water, the blood, and the Spirit, and the first of the witnesses that John mentions is water. Admittedly, verses 6-8 are hard to interpret. Most of the commentaries and scholars I have read say that the word "water" in verse 6 is referring to Christ's baptism. Some may see this as referring to Christ's physical birth, but I believe that in context, and for the sake of John's argument, that it makes more sense to interpret water as referring to Jesus' baptism by John the Baptist. So how does the baptism of Jesus testify to who He is?

To answer that question, let's look briefly at Matthew 3:13-17. Jesus' baptism is so important that it is recorded in all four gospels. In addition to Matthew 3, it is also recorded in Mark 1:9-11, Luke 3:21-23, and John 1:29-34, but they all consistently give the same account. Matthew 3:13-17 says:

"Then Jesus came from Galilee to John at the Jordan, to be baptized by him. But John tried to stop Him, saying, 'I need to be baptized by You, and yet You come to me?' Jesus answered him, 'Allow it for now, because this is the way for us to fulfill all righteousness." Then he allowed Him to be baptized. After Jesus was baptized, He went up immediately from the water. The heavens suddenly opened for Him, and He saw the Spirit of God descending like a dove and coming down on Him. And there came a voice from heaven: This is my beloved Son. I take delight in Him!"

Jesus showed up while John was baptizing at the Jordan river. Jesus asked John to baptize Him. At first John expressed hesitancy; after all, John's baptism was for repentance, and what did Jesus need to repent of? Nothing! That's why the idea of John baptizing Jesus was preposterous. But we see in this passage that God had a purpose. This baptism provided an opportunity for the true identity of Jesus to be revealed. It is a unique moment. Just picture in your mind what John and the people saw here: as Jesus came up from the water, the heavens open. That in and of itself is amazing. The portals of the invisible Kingdom of Heaven open, and for just a moment mere mortals get a small taste of the divine realm. As the heavens are opened, we see the Holy Spirit in the form of a dove descend on Christ.

Then the most amazing thing happens: God speaks! He declared Jesus to be the Son, and He expressed His divine delight in Him. All of the Trinity are present in this moment of commission for Jesus, and both the Spirit and the Father have testified and bore witness that Jesus is the Son, the second member of the Trinity.

This moment marks the beginning of Jesus' public earthly ministry. And in that moment, God testifies to His Son's deity. Baptism is also a moment of testimony for our own lives as believers. The word baptism means "to plunge or to immerse," and that is what we are doing at baptism. We are plunging into the water, being immersed completely, and coming out of the water. It is a demonstrative testimony of our new life in Christ. Wayne Grudem says going down into the water "...is a picture of going down into the grave and being buried. Coming out of the water is then a picture of being raised with Christ to walk in newness of life. Baptism thus very clearly pictures death to one's old way of life and rising to a new kind of life in Christ."[1] The act of baptism itself testifies to who we now are in Christ. We are dead to sin and alive with Christ. And just as the Trinity was present at Jesus' baptism, so we also baptize in the name of the Father, the Son, and the Holy Spirit. The baptism of a new believer in Christ is their first public testimony to who they now are. It is a beautiful picture and a powerful witness.

The Blood

The second witness John names in 1 John 6:6-8 is the blood, which is Christ's atoning death on the cross. So how does His death bear testimony

---

[1] Wayne Grudem, *Systematic Theology: An Introduction to Biblical Doctrine* (Grand Rapids, MI: Zondervan, 1994), 968-969

to who He is? Part of the answer to this question is found in the meaning of the word *atonement* itself. What Jesus actually accomplished on the cross is a testimony to who he was. So what is atonement? This is a deep question, and whole books have been written just on this topic alone. For our sake, I will simply define atonement this way: "a biblical doctrine that God has reconciled sinners to Himself through the sacrificial work of Jesus Christ."[2] We see many images and foreshadowings of Christ's atonement throughout the Bible. The idea is that of an exchange: In order for sinful man to be made right and reconciled to a holy God, something must be offered in his place. His sin must be atoned for in order to be accepted by God. And not just any sacrifice would do. Even in the Old Testament there were strict laws as to the type of sacrifice that was acceptable to God. None of the Old Testament images of atonement are clearer than that of the Day of Atonement mentioned in Leviticus 16. Once a year the High Priest of Israel would enter the Holy of Holies and offer a sacrifice on behalf of all the people for their sins. Before doing so, the High Priest had to first offer a sacrifice for Himself. How could he go before God and offer an atoning sacrifice for the people before first offering a sacrifice for his own sins? To go before God having not atoned for his own sin, the High Priest would instantly have died. God takes His holiness very seriously; therefore, the concept of atonement was very serious as well.

But the Bible is clear: Nothing the people ever did or nothing they ever could have offered, truly made them right with God. No matter how unblemished a sacrifice may have been, it wasn't good enough to permanently erase our sin and make us right with God. That is where Christ

---

[2] Chad Brand, Charles Draper, and Archie England, eds., "Atonement", in *Holman Illustrated Bible Dictionary* (Nashville, TN: Holman Bible Publishers, 2003), 139

comes in. He saw Himself as the fulfillment of all the Old Testament Law. He saw Himself as being that perfect sacrifice required for man's sin. But how do we know that God saw Jesus as the fulfilment of the atonement? The testimony of the cross bears witness to this: As Jesus died, He cried, "It is finished," (John 19:30). He saw His death as fulfilling the work the Father sent Him to do. Christ's testimony from the cross was that He had done everything needed to redeem His people and to atone for their sins.

There is also powerful testimony in the events surrounding the death of Jesus as recorded in Matthew 27. God demonstrated that the testimony of the cross was true by splitting the curtain of the sanctuary in two from top to bottom (v. 51), by sending a great earthquake (v. 51), and by opening the tombs of many saints who had previously died allowing them to walk around the city and be seen by many (vv. 52-53). We also know that a supernatural darkness came on the land during the middle of the day (Mark 15:33). You also see the centurion standing guard at the cross make a confession. He is witnessing the events surrounding Jesus' death and confesses, "This man really was God's Son!" (v.54). All these events and more bear witness to the fact that Jesus was the Son of God made flesh.

Of course, the most important and powerful witness to the validity of Christ's atonement was the empty tomb. By raising Jesus from the grave, God clearly testifies that Jesus is the Christ and the Son of God. His sacrifice has been accepted, and no more blood need be shed for the forgiveness of sin. That's why Paul can tell the people of Athens in Acts 17:30-31, "Therefore, having overlooked the times of ignorance, God now commands all people everywhere to repent, because He has set a day when He is going to judge the world in righteousness by the Man He has appointed. He has provided proof of this to everyone by raising Him from the dead."

Just as we follow Christ's footsteps in making a public testimony in baptism, so we testify to the truth of the atonement in the ordinance of the Lord's Supper. By taking the bread and wine, we testify that the death of Christ was enough. When we take the bread, we acknowledge that His body was broken for us. When we take the cup, we confess that His blood was shed for our sins. Through the ordinance of the Lord's Supper, we declare that the death of Christ has cleansed us from sin, and we invite sinners to be reconciled to God through the shed blood of Christ. I love how Mark Dever speaks of the atonement:

"Historically understood, Christ's atonement gives hope to Christians in their sin and in their suffering. If we have any assurance of salvation, it is because of Christ's atonement; if any joy, it flows from Christ's work on the cross. The atonement protects us from our naïve tendency to replace religion with morality and God's grace with legalism. Apart from Christ's atoning work, we would be forever guilty, ashamed, and condemned before God."[3]

The Spirit

The final witness in this group is the Spirit. The Spirit has come convicting us of sin, indwelling in our hearts, and reminding us of the words of Jesus. These facts validate the testimony of Christ. In John 15:26, Jesus promised His disciples that the Holy Spirit would come. He said, "When the Counselor comes, the One I will send to you from the Father-- the Spirit of

---

[3] J.I. Packer and Mark Dever, *In My Place Condemned He Stood: Celebrating the Glory of the* Atonement (Wheaton, IL: Crossway, 2007), 102

truth who proceeds from the Father-- He will testify about Me." The Holy Spirit by His very nature testifies to who Jesus is, and the Holy Spirit, being God, cannot lie. Therefore, all of His testimony regarding Jesus is true.

Every time we are convicted of sin, we are reminded of the truth of Jesus' claims. Every time we sense supernatural joy welling up in our hearts, we are reminded that, just as Jesus promised, the Holy Spirit is at work in our lives. Every time we speak the truth and testify to who Jesus is, the Holy Spirit is there guiding our thoughts and giving us courage. When God's people meet corporately and praise God together, the Holy Spirit is there among us testifying that God is with us and that Jesus is the Messiah. At times when we are silent in prayer because we don't know what to say, the Holy Spirit testifies with our spirit, praying on our behalf. The Holy Spirit's job is to be an internal witness in every believer that Jesus is the Christ and the Son of the living God. The Spirit's job is to shine a spotlight on Jesus, and what an amazing, reliable, and trustworthy witness He is.

In verse 8, John says that the water, the blood, and the Spirit are all in agreement that Jesus is the Son of God in the flesh. This is referring to Deuteronomy 17:6, which states that no one can be condemned to capital punishment without the testimony of two to three witnesses. The witness of the water, the blood, and the Spirit more than satisfy this demand. But that is not all. There are still three more witnesses to testify.

The Witness of the Father and the Believer (5:9-10)

The Father

I think one of the most beautiful relationships you see in Scripture is the divine relationship between the Father and the Son. The Bible is very clear: God delights in his Son. No one knows the Son like the Father.

Jesus is the beloved Son. In Isaiah 42:1, God speaks of his Son this way, "This is My Servant, I strengthen Him, this is My Chosen One; I delight in Him." In 1 John 5:9, John presents the Father as the most powerful witness of all.

John is making an argument here: If we are willing to receive the testimony of men, how much greater is God's testimony? In a court of law, if multiple witnesses come forth and speak to the truth of something and individually corroborate the truth, we believe them. Their words can either acquit or condemn someone. If we accept the validity of two or three witnesses to decide matters on earth, ought not God's testimony be accepted all the more?

God has provided ample evidence that Jesus is His Son. Other than audibly declaring it at both Jesus' baptism and the Transfiguration, He has also left us the historical, eye-witness accounts of Jesus in the Gospels. Every time Jesus performed a miracle, God was testifying about the power of His Son. When Jesus spoke words of rebuke to a storm and it listened and stopped, God was testifying that Jesus was His beloved Son. When Jesus called Lazarus by name from his grave, the power and testimony of God was on display, clearly saying, "This is my Son!" Even demons bowed in obedience to Jesus. Who else but the Son of God has the power to command Satan's legions? The God-given historical record of the life of Jesus is God's testimony to us that Jesus is the unique Son of God.

It should be clear to us that God has testified both to the truth of who Jesus is as His unique Son, and He has declared His delight in Jesus, the beloved Son. And with the Holy Spirit's help, the same delight that God has for the Son will be in us, too. To quote John Piper:

"If God's pleasure in the Son becomes our pleasure, then the object of our pleasure, Jesus, will be inexhaustible in personal worth. He will never become boring or disappointing or frustrating. No greater treasure can be conceived than the Son of God...God's delight in His Son will be in us and it will be ours. And this will never end, because neither the Father nor the Son ever ends." [4]

The Believer

John says something very interesting in 6:10: those who believe in Jesus as the Son of God have a testimony within them. When we confess Jesus with our mouths, God makes that confession a reality in our hearts. God's Spirit works in us to testify to the truth about Jesus. Romans 8:16 says, "The Spirit Himself testifies together with our spirit that we are God's children."

So this testimony is an internal testimony in every believer. Isn't it true that sometimes you need to be reminded of the love of God for you? But isn't it great to know that you don't have to look to an outside source for that reminder? God has put a constant everyday reminder in you with the gift of His Spirit. It daily bears internal testimony to our hearts of who Jesus is and who we are in Him. We can know for sure that we belong to God because of this internal witness.

This verse also comes with a warning to those who would refuse the testimony of God regarding His So: to reject God's testimony about Jesus is to call God a liar. God, as we just learned, has testified to the truth of who

---

[4] John Piper, *The Pleasures of God: Meditations on God's Delight in Being God* (Sisters, OR: Multnomah Publishers, 2000), 27

Jesus is. But many false teachers of John's day were calling God a liar in rejecting Jesus as His Son. They were denying the full humanity of Jesus.

It is the same today: Anyone who would deny any aspect of who Jesus is, as revealed to us by Scripture, is calling God a liar. We are called to accept the testimony of God about Jesus. Anything less than that-- or more than that-- is false teaching and should be rejected. Danny Akin again says it well when he states, "John says that believing in Jesus as the Son of God is equivalent to accepting the Father's testimony about His Son. To reject Jesus as God's Son is the equivalent to charging God with perjury."[5]

The Witness of Eternal Life (5:11-12)

A message that you get very loud and clear from John throughout this whole letter is that to have Jesus is to have eternal life. It is also clear from this passage that eternal life is a gift of God. It isn't something you earn or can purchase; it is part of God's gift to those who trust in Christ. To have Jesus is to have eternal life. This isn't simply life unending; it is so much more. Jesus the Son is by his very nature eternal. To be granted eternal life, therefore, is to participate in the very eternality of Jesus. As He even now is eternal, we also as believers have been granted the blessing of participating in the eternal life of Jesus.

This is the sum of the testimony concerning Christ. The gift of eternal life testifies to the fact that Jesus is God, and as such He is eternal. He is the endless fountain of life itself. By imparting that to those who

---

[5] Daniel L. Akin, *Christ-Centered Exposition: Exalting Jesus in 1, 2, and 3 John*, eds. David Platt, Daniel L. Akin, and Tony Merida (Nashville, TN: B&H Publishing Group, 2014), 134

believe, He gives witness to the fact that He is the Son. This is a word of assurance for those who follow Jesus: eternal life is ours now! Because we are in Christ, we have eternal life right now. We can be assured that to be in Christ means that even now we are participating in the eternal life of Christ. While it is true that even believers will face physical death one day, we can be assured that because we are in Christ we have been granted eternal life and death will not be the end. Heaven and a new, eternal body await those who trust in Christ.

There is also a warning here. Verse 12 is very clear that to not have the Son is to not possess eternal life. See, there is something worse than physical death, and that is spiritual death. We will all spend eternity somewhere. To face eternity without Christ is to face it with not only the certainty of physical death but eternal spiritual death as well. If true eternal life can be found only in Christ, then to die without Him is to face what the Bible calls "the second death," (Revelation 20:14-15). This is why it is so vitally important that we as believers continue to share the gospel. There are still many without Christ. They have no hope of eternal life; therefore, only the prospect of eternal death without Him awaits. We bear witness to Jesus and the eternal life that only He can give when we share the gospel with others. We must continue to call people everywhere to repent and turn to Christ because only the Eternal Son can grant eternal life.

In a world of uncertainty and chaos, the people of God stand and defend the certain testimony about Christ. Every time we baptize a new believer, we are testifying to the fact that God is still granting eternal life to those who would die to their old way of life and trust Christ. Every time the body of Christ gathers in participation of the Lord's Supper, we are testifying to the atoning death of Christ. We are declaring to the world that the blood of Christ, and only the blood of Christ, can cleanse us from sin and make us right with God. We are also reminding ourselves of just what it cost God to offer us salvation.

In a world full of uncertainty, it is easy to begin to allow doubt to creep into our hearts. But it is in these moments that the unfailing love of God shines through. He has given us the internal testimony of His Spirit, who daily reminds us of the goodness and grace of God for sinners. He continually reminds us of the words of Jesus and assures our troubled hearts of the eternal life found only in Christ.

Nothing is certain in this life except one thing: the unfailing love the Father has for the Son and for those who have trusted Him as Savior. Let's remind ourselves daily of the sure testimony of who Jesus is, and let's bear witness to the water, the blood, and the Spirit. Let us read God's Word and fully embrace the Father's testimony regarding His Son. Let's let our transformed lives bear testimony to the grace of God found in Christ Jesus the Son. And let's proclaim eternal life found only in Christ as long as we live.

Chapter 13| What We Can Know
1 John 5:13-20

I mentioned early in this book that one of the early church heresies that John and the Apostles all dealt with was an early form of what became known as Gnosticism. Gnosticism was a combination of many different ancient teachings which would eventually also include Christianity. For instance, it would combine Jewish and Christian beliefs with ancient Greek philosophy. The name Gnosticism is derived from the Greek word *ginosko* or *gnosis* which means to know or to understand. John Macarthur says this about gnostic teaching:

> The general emphasis of Gnostic teaching was special spiritual knowledge. They taught that matter (the physical universe, e.g., the body) was inherently evil while spirit (the spiritual world, e.g., the mind) was good. That division between the spiritual and physical led them to believe that the height of religious activity was carried out in the mind. The body, and what one did with the body, was

irrelevant to Gnostic religion. Therefore, Gnosticism was the pursuit of esoteric, mysterious spiritual knowledge, while the body and the physical world were disregarded and ignored.

That philosophical dualism caused them to be indifferent to moral values and ethical behavior. To them, the body and spirit were completely distinct. So much so, in fact, that sin committed by the body had no connection to or effect on the spirit. Obtaining the special, mysterious knowledge allowed a person to totally divorce himself from anything earthly, anything physical, and anything behavioral.

In fact, as long as you had that special knowledge, it wasn't important that the particulars of your theology were correct. It didn't matter what you believed about God, Christ, and the Holy Spirit, as long as you had your secret knowledge."[1]

John combats this false teaching all throughout his letter. That is why John focuses so much on Christ coming in the flesh (See Chapter 12 of this book). He also uses some form of the Greek word for "know" twenty-seven times. John, in his concluding thoughts in this letter, wanted God's people to understand that they could indeed know God, they could know who Jesus is, and they could know how that knowledge impacts them and how to live it out. Knowledge of God isn't locked away in a vault somewhere only to be obtained by those who gained the spiritual secrets to this grand mystery. Knowledge of God is revealed to us in the person of Christ and in the pages of His holy Word.

---

[1] John MacArthur, "Reviving an Ancient Lie," Grace to You, published June 12, 2014, https://www.gty.org/library/blog/B140612/reviving-an-ancient-lie.

That is what we will look at in this chapter. There are five truths John wants God's people to know from this passage in 1 John. Let's look at them all individually.

We Have Eternal Life (5:13)

In this verse, John sums up one of the main truths he wants God's people to know beyond a shadow of a doubt: in Christ they have eternal life. One dictionary defines eternal life as, "life at its best, having infinite duration characterized by abiding fellowship with God."[2] John wanted believers to have confidence in their eternal inheritance. He wanted believers to know that, in spite of all the opposition the church may face in this life and in spite of all the suffering that saints have endured throughout the generations, the assurance of eternal life awaits.

This is something we can know. John uses two Greek words for "know" in this passage. The one used in 1 John 5:13 is *eido*. This word is also translated in other places as "to see". We can examine and inspect and perceive this truth with the eyes of our hearts. We can hold it and know it and cherish this truth. We can trust that there is certainty in the promises of God. When He says that all those who repent and come to Christ will have eternal life, He means it. God can promise that because He is powerful enough to bring it to fruition. He not only promises that we can have eternal life, but He promises that He will be with us throughout the duration of eternity (Revelation 21:3). To have eternal life in Christ is to be granted eternal access to the presence of God. It is to spend eternity beholding and

---

[2] Chad Brand, Charles Draper, and Archie England, eds., "Eternal Life", in *Holman Illustrated Bible Dictionary* (Nashville, TN: Holman Bible Publishers, 2003), 511

delighting in His glory. It means we will have eternal, unbroken fellowship with our Savior.

What is the primary joy of heaven? It is God Himself. Randy Alcorn says that, "God's glory will be the air we breathe, and we'll always breathe deeper to gain more of it. In the new universe, we'll never be able to travel far enough to leave God's presence. If we could, we'd never want to. However great the wonders of Heaven, God Himself is Heaven's greatest prize."[3]

So the promise of eternal life and the promise of being in heaven with God go hand in hand. John MacArthur wrote a wonderful book about this truth called *The Glory of Heaven: The Truth About Heaven, Angels, and Eternal Life*. In it, he says that heaven, the place of eternal life, is, "...a place where the riches of God's grace shine even more brightly than they do here on earth...Heaven will be an eternity of God pouring out His kindness on His beloved children!" He goes on to say that, "every good thing we know here on earth is a product of God's grace. And we who know Christ are going to heaven for this express purpose: so that God can showcase the infinite riches of His grace by showering His goodness on us endlessly. Does that not make your heart prefer the riches of heaven to the meager pleasures of earth?"[4]

I think that is what John is trying to get the church to see here. Yes, things are hard here on earth. Yes, the church must endure much suffering, scorn, and ridicule. Yes, many will die as martyrs for the sake of the gospel. But the hope of eternal life and the certainty of eternal fellowship with Christ is more precious that a comfortable life here and now. The reason

---

[3] Randy Alcorn, *Heaven* (Carol Stream, IL: Tyndale House Publishers, 2004), 185
[4] John MacArthur, *The Glory of Heaven: The Truth About Heaven, Angels, and Eternal Life* (Wheaton, IL: Crossway, 1996), 87

that the promise of eternal salvation is so reassuring for believers is that it helps us see past the darkness of this life to the bright glory of the eternal one to come. And that truth and assurance should stir our hearts daily.

God Answers Prayer (5:14-17)

The next truth that John wants believers to know is that God delights in hearing and answering the prayers of His children. John repeats here a truth he taught in 1 John 3 that we can have boldness and confidence before the throne of God. This confidence has nothing to do with us or how righteous we are. The reason we can have confidence before God isn't based on our merits but on the merits of Christ. I spoke of this confidence in depth in chapter 8 of this book, but here in this chapter I mostly want to highlight what it means to ask or pray according to the will of God.

John says in 5:14-15 that if we ask anything according to God's will, we can know He hears us, and we can have what we ask. Now, we know God doesn't always give us everything we ask of Him. Sometimes this makes us angry in the moment. It makes us feel like God isn't listening. But often, in retrospect, we become very grateful that God did not answer that prayer and give us exactly what we asked. As a matter of fact, for some of us it is very troubling to think about the things we formerly asked of God. We see that often our prayers can be self-centered or materialistic. So what does it mean to ask according to God's will? That is an important question because according to John you will receive anything you ask in accordance with God's will.

It is clear that John is giving a command here. He is telling believers they can have confidence in prayer if they ask according to God's will. God can do anything we ask of Him. He is all powerful and there is nothing He can't do except sin. He won't act contrary to his holy character. When we pray, it is not a question of "Does God have the power to do what we ask?" but "Will He?"

Matthew Henry says, "Our prayers must always be offered in submission to the will of God."[5] How do we know what the will of God is, and how do we align our prayers with His will? Paul, I believe, answers this question in Romans 12:1-2 when he says, "Therefore, brothers, by the mercies of God, I urge you to present your bodies as a living sacrifice, holy and pleasing to God; this is your spiritual worship. Do not be conformed to this age, but be transformed by the renewing of your mind, so that you may discern what is the good, pleasing, and perfect will of God." Paul makes three very important points about God's will in this passage. First, God's will is good; it is pleasing and joyful. Secondly, God's will is pleasing. Some translations use the word "acceptable" here. So God's will is good for us, and it should be acceptable and pleasing to us. Lastly, Paul says that God's will is perfect; His will is complete and lacking nothing.

Paul is saying that in order to understand God's will, and thus to pray according to it, we must offer ourselves daily to God. We submit ourselves to Him. We dig deep into His revealed word. As His Spirit works in us to expose sin and bring a deeper understanding of who God is, we begin to more fully and clearly understand His will. As we submit to Him, he breaks all the things in us that still cling to and conform to this world. He transforms our hearts and minds to bring them into alignment with His will. So understanding God's will is a daily process. It is continually submitting

---

[5] Matthew Henry, "1 John 5:13-17", from *Matthew Henry's Concise Commentary*, Bible Hub, Accessed August 19, 2020, https://biblehub.com/commentaries/1_john/5-14.htm.

yourself to Him and His word, and as you do He transforms the way you think. This affects our prayer life: The more we understand God, and the more we understand His will, the more we will ask for things that align with His will.

That's what John means here in 5:14-15. We learn to discern the will of God, and we ask for things in accordance with His will. When we do this, God graciously hears our prayers, and He will mercifully grant us anything we ask according to His will.

John then gives an example of this kind of confident prayer life in 5:16-17. The example of prayer you see in these two verses is what is called intercession: It is praying to God on behalf of someone else. John is wanting to imagine a fellow believer who is dealing with sin. It is important that this sin is not one that "leads to death" as John puts it. In other words, it isn't an unforgivable sin. Even believers struggle with sin, and John is saying we should intercede for them according to the will of God. It is good and right to pray that God would restore and lead to repentance a brother or sister caught in sin.

But what is the sin leading to death? It could be someone who is sinning willfully and deliberately, which is not in accordance with being a believer at all. Thus, they are still lost and on their way to eternal death. It could also be someone speaking blasphemy against the Holy Spirit. It is possible John is also referring to someone who just outright rejects the gospel. Either way, John isn't saying not to pray for them, but prayer for one who so blatantly and willfully commits these types of sins isn't likely to change this person because they have committed a sin John says leads to death. The main thing to pray for in these circumstances, I believe, is that

God would divinely intervene in their life, reveal to them the truth of gospel, and bring them to repentance.

Here is what we can know: When we pray according to the will of God, He hears us. That is a wonderful truth. The God of the universe is not too busy to hear the honest and earnest prayers of His people. He loves His children and delights in their prayers.

We Can Overcome Sin (5:18)

John makes what seems to be a shocking and startling statement in 5:18: those who are born of God and belong to Him do not sin. I do not think John is talking about sinless perfection here. Ongoing and unrepentant sin is not the pattern of life for a believer. God in His infinite mercy and grace has broken the power of sin in our lives. Sin is no longer our habit or pattern; holiness is. We may not be able to be perfect in this life, but we can be pure.

In this life, a believer still struggles with sin, but we do not fight it alone. John says that those born of God are kept by God. God's power is working in us assisting us in our fight against sin. God will keep those who are born of Him. He will not see them fall back into the power of sin. As believers, it is important that we have the mindset of overcomers when it comes to sin. Sin has been defeated. Whereas once we were slaves to sin, we are no longer bound by it. By the power and grace of God we have overcome it.

Not only have we overcome the power of sin, but John says we have overcome the power of Satan as well. This doesn't mean that Satan does not affect us at all or that he doesn't still have power to tempt believers.

What I think John is speaking of here is that for those in Christ, Satan can no longer lay hold of them to do them harm. Satan is not all-powerful. His work is limited by the sovereignty of God. He can't do anything without God's permission. Satan stands to accuse God's people every day, but our good and sovereign God keeps us secure by His limitless power.

We, as His people, are still so prone to wander. We fail to grasp the immensity of God's love for us. When times get uncertain, many of us would flee back to lesser pleasures in order to find solace. But God in His unfailing love keeps us from returning to the muck of our past life of sin. He daily helps us overcome sin and Satan, and He does that because we belong to Him.

We Belong to God (5:19)

This is the fourth certainty for the believer. We belong to God. Think deeply on that sentence for a minute. This truth is really the foundation for all of the other certainties we've talked about so far. We can know that we have eternal life, we can have confidence in prayer, and we can be sure that we have overcome the power of sin all because of this one reality: we belong to God.

John says that those born of God are of God. What does it mean to be "of God?" I'm using the word *belong* here because I think that is what John is conveying. But in the Greek, the word "of" in verse 19 denotes origin. It means "to proceed from or to come out of something." John is saying is that those who belong to God proceed from God. They proceed from Him. We are his possession. And John makes it clear in this passage that there are only two types of people in this world: those who are of God and who belong to Him and those who are under the sway of Satan. There is no in-between. You either belong to God now or you don't. God doesn't take possession of His children when they die; He possesses them even now. This is a certainty, and it should bring us comfort. To belong to God is to no longer be under the influence of Satan or the world.

Dear Christian, you belong to God! Praise the Lord for that! You are His. He has paid the price for your redemption. He has given you new life. He hears your prayers. Even now He is preparing you for life eternal with Him. If you are in Christ, you are possessed by the almighty maker of heaven and earth. He is yours, and you are His.

Many people struggle with belonging in this world. There are so many lost souls searching for a place to call their own. Many believers feel this way too, and that is okay. We shouldn't feel at home in this world. We belong to another world. If anyone holds out to you a secret to belonging in this world, he or she is a false teacher. To be in Christ is to find that you are not of this world. You will always feel out of place. But we can find solace in the fact that we belong to God. And if we belong to Him, we can be certain that one day He will bring us to our home where we do belong. What a powerful image! We belong to God, and Satan has no hold on us!

We Can Know Jesus, the True One (5:20)

Of all the things that John wants his dear children to know, He wants them to know Christ most of all. The Son has come, and His name is Jesus. Jesus has come and has given us understanding. The wonderful mystery of Christianity is that God didn't sit and wait for His people to find them. He isn't hoping that in their endless search for meaning and purpose that maybe they'll stumble upon His reality. The wonder of Christianity is that God the Son temporarily left his place in heaven and came down to earth and made Himself known. In Christ, God has made Himself known.

This truth is the foundation of all other Christian belief and practice so that we may know Christ. Specifically, John wants the church to know that Jesus is the True One, He is the Son of the Father, and He is the Christ.

What a beautiful truth to conclude with! In a world of uncertainty, knowing Christ makes all the difference in the world. He is our salvation. He is our propitiation and atonement. He is the exact expression of God and the radiance of His glory. He is the embodiment of truth and love. He has conquered sin and death by His own death and resurrection. He purchased His Bride with His own blood, and He is working even now to purify her. And one day He will bring her home to experience eternal fellowship with Him.

This world is uncertain and ever-changing. But it is also fading. It will not last. There is only one thing that is unchanging, and that is God Himself. Love for the things of this world lead to destruction and heartache, but the unfailing love of God will sustain His people now and forever.

Conclusion| Be On Guard for Idols
1 John 5:21

You may have read that last chapter and said, "Wait a minute. He didn't cover verse 21." No, I didn't; I felt it needed its own space. I also felt it a fitting conclusion to this book. John spent the bulk of his letter expounding upon the excellences of Christ and encouraging believers to live out their faith. But there were also plenty of warnings to avoid what John called "antichrists," false teachers opposed to the work of Christ and His church. So it seems fitting that John would conclude his letter with one final warning.

Again, he leads with his affection for the church. His fatherly love for the church overflows all over this letter. He is an elderly man by this point in his life, so when he calls them "little children" you know that he is speaking in earnest love for them. He warns them to stay on guard against idols. If Jesus is the one True God, then it is implied that many false gods abound vying for the attention and affection of the church. Many of the believers who were part of the church in John's day were Gentiles. They came from pagan backgrounds where the worship of false gods was the norm. They were probably tempted to return to them when times got tough for the early church, but John is reminding them to cling to what he has taught them.

This warning is no less stark for believers in the twenty-first century. Although many of us were not raised in paganism and did not have images or idols in our homes, we still have the ability to fashion idols for ourselves in times of trouble and tribulation. Idols can take many forms. The secular idols of rugged individualism, materialism, humanism, post-modernism, and theological liberalism are prevalent all around the United States. They would all seek to lead Christians down false paths, making false promises, and distorting the true gospel along the way. These are all man-centered and not God-centered at their heart.

If we are to survive uncertain times, then the hope of the true gospel is our only consolation. It tells us that all things are working together for good for those who love Christ. It tells us that there is a better tomorrow coming where sin in banished, death is no more, and Christ will reign and rule for all eternity. The true gospel tells us that this life isn't all there is. Evil and uncertainty and depression and hopelessness do not have the final say for those who trust Christ.

That is why all idols must be crushed: they just simply don't measure up. They don't provide hope, certainty, or salvation. Those truths are only found in the person of Jesus Christ. He was the Word at the beginning, He was and is the eternal Son, He is our atonement and propitiation, and He is coming back again.

Dear Christian, stand against the tide of the current culture and proclaim Jesus until He returns. Flee to Him in uncertain days. His love never fails, His grace never runs out, and His mercy is new every day. What in this world can possibly compare to that?

Children of God, guard yourselves from idols!

About the Author

J Ryan Wicker is currently serving as Associate Pastor of Education at First Baptist Church Dickson, TN. He received his MA in Theological Studies from The Southern Baptist Theological Seminary in Louisville, Ky. He has been happily married to his wife of 15 years, Rebekah. Together they have three children: Madie, John, and Emmett.

If you are interested in group study materials for

Unfailing Love in Uncertain Times: A Journey

Through 1 John

Please visit https://www.fbcdickson.org/news/e-book-resources- for a free

study guide

Made in the USA
Coppell, TX
05 August 2021